HOOKED ON LANGUAGES!

HOOKED ON LANGUAGES!

READY-TO-USE VISUAL ACTIVITIES FOR LEARNING FOREIGN LANGUAGES

PENILYN KRUGE

Illustrations by Ellen J. Emerson

THE CENTER FOR APPLIED RESEARCH IN EDUCATION
West Nyack, New York 10995

10 9 8 7 6 5 4 3 2

Library of Congress Cataloging-in-Publication Data

Kruge, Penilyn H.
    Hooked on Languages! : ready-to-use visual activities for learning foreign lan-
guages / Penilyn H. Kruge.
        p. cm.
    ISBN 0-87628-412-8
    1. Language and languages—Studying and teaching—Audio-visual aids..
I. Title.
P53.2.K78   1996
418′.0078—dc20   95-20712
                                                                    CIP

Jacqueline Roulette, Production Editor
Interior Design by William Ruoto

ISBN 0-87628-412-8

**THE CENTER FOR APPLIED RESEARCH
IN EDUCATION**
West Nyack, NY 10994
A Simon & Schuster Company

On the World Wide Web at http://www.phdirect.com

Printed in the United States of America

DEDICATION

Each academic subject has its own challenges as teachers try to convey information to students of all ability and interest levels, so that they comprehend, then apply, what they have learned. Learning a foreign language is one such challenge.

The foreign language teacher is faced with many dimensions of foreign language teaching, as well as a multitude of emotional responses to the subject—the whole gamut from love to hate, with a large amount of indifference in between. While teaching the exciting, eye-and-mind opening cultural lessons on one day, the foreign language teacher struggles with lurking anxiety about the next day's return to the rigors of vocabulary and grammar lessons.

Forcing students to make unfamiliar sounds, from which they are supposed to derive meaning, is a battle. The class period is usually not devoted to free discussion of a theme. Instead, the class is masterfully directed by the teacher who has planned a host of explanations, drills, and contrived conversational setups. So, to this diligent craftsperson, the language teacher, I dedicate my attempts to ease the job of enticing language learners to work seriously with you, to learn effectively, and—it is hoped—to enjoy the process.

ACKNOWLEDGMENTS

To all my students who inspired me

To all my friends who assisted and encouraged me

To all interested language teachers

To Ellen Emerson, my friend and expert illustrator

To Ronald Zuckerman, my friend and greatest encourager

ABOUT THE AUTHOR

Penilyn Kruge has taught public school for 22 years as a foreign language teacher in Bergen County, New Jersey. During her first five years she taught French, Spanish, and German at Park Ridge High School, and in the ensuing 17 years she taught French and Spanish at Pascack Hills High School in Montvale, New Jersey. The author is listed in the 1994 edition of *Who's Who Among America's Teachers*. Living in Europe as a child and as an adult, with exposure to many different systems of education from elementary to university level, imbued Ms. Kruge not only with an appreciation for foreign cultures, but also with an awareness of the great diversity in teaching expectations and methodologies.

After a B.A. from Wheaton College (Illinois) and an M.A. from N.Y.U., Ms. Kruge continued taking courses and seminars at many colleges and universities both in the United States and abroad. Her perpetual quest is for the continued improvement of instruction for more effective learning.

One of the most important considerations is that of the varied learning modalities of students. Whereas some respond better to auditory teaching, and others to kinesthetic, many others respond to visual presentations. With the new generation of learners, a visual approach, combined with the other learning channels, provides the most effective learning for the largest number of students; thus the creation of *Hooked on Languages!*

ABOUT THIS BOOK

Those of us who have taught for many years have undoubtedly noticed changes in the learning habits and patterns of students. Certain rigors that we previously required of our students are, for various reasons, difficult to exact. The bottom line is that we must adapt to our students' learning modes as they learn the material dictated by the curriculum.

The goals for teaching foreign languages have changed over the years. More practical expectations are delineated in the course curriculum. Enticing students to use the target language is of utmost importance. To use the language, students must first get it, in the sense of acquiring it. Acquisition of the usable elements of language is the focus of the activities in *Hooked on Languages!*

LEARNING STYLES

One of the most important features in teaching is respecting the different learning styles of our students. While some students favor auditory learning, others favor kinesthetic, and others visual. The current generation of students has been exposed to great amounts of visual learning, or at least, visual stimuli, thus this text uses a visual image as a stepping stone to first comprehending the material that ultimately should be mastered orally.

Remembering back to the presentation of the ETRE house to learn the passé composé in French, I recall how much easier it was to learn in a visual manner rather than to memorize a list. My own experience in teaching validates the success of representing language elements in a visual manner, buttressed by auditory and oral work, thus relying on many learning strengths. The initial visual presentation makes the obscure graspable, and lessens the degree of abstraction—thus lessening the degree of anxiety. When the old "grammar-speak" is incomprehensible, like a foreign language itself to our students, an image gives students a framework within which to crystallize their understanding of a concept, to differentiate it from others, and to retrieve the information as needed.

With acquisition of the language as our goal, we must engage the attention level of our students to the highest degree possible. Leading students to focus on a given topic, especially that of a dry grammatical explanation, is a major challenge in itself. A visual image enables students to focus on the concept at hand, the parameters of what is to be learned, and to learn it well. In classrooms where there are great disparities in learning abilities, this approach helps to narrow the gap.

AFFECTIVE LEARNING

The power of the affective response to learning a subject must be considered; thus it would behoove us to present the material as simply and in as minimalist a manner as possible. Once the basic kernels of information are grasped, and the student is not overwhelmed by the tidal waves of exceptions to all rules, then the more minute rules can be presented. A type of triage is carried out with respect to grammatical rules in *Hooked on Languages!* The most used or the most important are isolated and drilled until students are comfortable with them. Encasing the rules in an image gives boundaries to the students to aid in their understanding. In fact, one of the drawbacks of this approach is that the students develop such a cocky sense of security that they don't feel a need to study or even to refresh their memory before a test or quiz!

VISUAL PRESENTATION SUGGESTIONS

Suggestions for a visual presentation of grammar and vocabulary are made for the initial presentation of a topic, for the recapitulation of it, for chapter or test review, as well as for class and homework assignments.

All of the suggestions in *Hooked on Languages!* are routine presentations in my own language classes. They are merely suggestions—with the hope that you, as teachers, will feel challenged to see new images of your own that will work even more effectively. If you think that you lack the creativity to do so, throw the challenge to your students.

In fact, when I have asked volunteers to present to the class my visual lesson on a particular concept, for review and for instruction to the students who were absent on the initial presentation day, the students invariably repeated my lesson, image for image, then embellished the images. Their own creativity became a welcome addition. Learning from their peers-turned-teachers added entertainment, amusement, and attention to the concept being highlighted, thus reinforcing it. With "cooperative learning" as a contemporary educational buzzword, teaching via images is a useful tool for such learning.

Most of the visual diagrams pertain to grammatical concepts for Spanish classes, reflecting the fact that most of my classes have been in this area. Some pertain to French, many to both languages, and many, especially those in the vocabulary section, can be adapted to other languages. Again, they are merely suggestions as to how visual presentations can work for more effective learning.

Written specifically for today's foreign language teacher, *Hooked on Languages!* especially helps the teacher who feels challenged by students who are easily distracted, those of short attention spans, those who prefer "doing," those who need to understand what they are doing, and those who do not learn languages well from lists.

It is sincerely hoped that you will freely reproduce the visual diagrams—and add to them.

Finally, develop a policy of "postponement." Like a steeping tea bag, words and concepts need time to sink in. An incubation period is needed to allow time for interaction and integration of the new knowledge with the existing infrastructure. Words and concepts need constant drill to the point of saturation. Presenting new material today, then testing it tomorrow is an injustice to students. They need time to work with the material—perhaps days, perhaps a week. Consider postponing the quiz or test until students show a sense of comfort and mastery.

Penilyn Kruge

HOW TO USE THE VISUAL DIAGRAMS

Each concept or activity (such as a chapter review) is centered around a visual diagram that can be used as an overhead transparency, copied at the chalkboard, and/or reproduced for student use—the way they were initially presented in my classes before I chose to make a permanent collection of the ideas. The pages are meant to be copied, then made into visual diagrams, preferably colored ones. The pages may have to be photocopied first, before the thermofax machine can make a legible overhead copy. Different-colored washable pens help enhance student interest. Nonpermanent overhead pens are vital because the material must be erased, then rewritten to test for comprehension of the major point of the lesson.

A page or more is devoted to explaining how to use each visual diagram, step by step. Included within these explanations are exercises intended for oral drills, both choral and individual, that are essential support in the learning process. Each step of the drill activity should be mastered before proceeding to the next step. In most cases, a blank diagram is included for you to use immediately, with samples of completed visual diagrams to show the process or end result.

What can be done for students who are absent? A student volunteer can be called upon to re-explain your visual diagram to the class. This provides learning for the absentees, review for the students who were in class, and a chance at leadership for the volunteers. Students are at times more willing to accept teaching from peers than from their teachers. An option for absent students is the use of a peer who could, in the spirit of cooperative learning, teach the returning absentees in another area of the classroom while the teacher continues the lesson.

It is suggested that the homework assignment on the first night following the initial presentation be closely aligned with the oral drills.

CONTENTS

Drawn by Kevin Standler

Anyone who has taken a class with Ms. Kruge can verify that her teaching methods are different from the traditional ones used by many teachers. She is aware that people have different learning channels: visual, auditory, verbal, and kinesthetic. Her instructional techniques cater to these various learning styles. Whether by singing vocabulary words or competing in a "speed and accuracy" drill, clearly Ms. Kruge knows the latest scoop on teaching languages. Her book, *Hooked on Languages!* is a teacher's guide of effective methods to teach language, mainly Spanish, but the visual approach is applicable to all languages. Ms. Kruge's philosophy is similar to the old adage—"I hear and I forget. I see and I remember. I do and I understand."

The Wrangler, 1995

Pascack Hills High School Yearbook

 comparatives

 tenses

Part One

GRAMMAR

 plurals

 prepositions

 pronouns

PRONOUNS

FACE: Object Pronouns, Direct vs. Indirect

Prior to teaching the difference between direct and indirect object pronouns, the teacher should teach the "Thing System" with a direct object pronoun as it applies to a thing—the most common translation of which is "it." Drill specifically the third person singular pronouns with many different kinds of verbs. Once this has been learned it will be time to present the "People System," with direct and indirect object pronouns.

It has always been a particularly difficult task to teach students the difference between the direct and indirect object pronouns, especially since so many students do not have a grasp of the concept in their own language. A visual framework gives students an image to summon up when they are called upon to know the difference in the pronouns.

HOW TO USE THE VISUAL DIAGRAM

1. Briefly explain to the students that indirect object pronouns are used with verbs that communicate a message, thus using two special parts of the body—the hand and the mouth.

2. Elicit from the students the target language verbs that emanate from the hand; write them across the hand on the overhead transparency made from the visual diagram. Then drill in a sentence with the third person singular pronoun, in the target language. Refer to the following exercises:

    I <u>give</u> him.   Do you <u>write</u> to her?

    He <u>does</u> her <u>a favor</u>.   She <u>lends</u> him her book.

    We <u>borrow</u> from her.   They <u>show</u> him.

    He <u>sends</u> her a rose.   She <u>buys</u> him a shirt.

3. Next, elicit verbs that emanate from the mouth, verbs used with people. Drill these in the same way as in the previous examples. The verb "to telephone" or "to call" may be an exception to the rule, depending upon the foreign language; thus it would have to be pointed out separately.

    I <u>speak</u> to him.   Do you <u>yell</u> at him?

    He <u>reads</u> to her.   She <u>sings</u> to him.

    We <u>answer</u> him.   They <u>ask</u> her.

4. Now it is time to move on to the direct object pronouns. Using the third person singular pronouns (alternate with masculine and feminine), elicit the verbs emanating from the eye, and drill. Proceed to the verbs which emanate from the ear and drill. Always write the verbs as close to the body part as possible. Proceed to the nose (or avoid this part of the body), the heart, then the brain.

eye: I <u>watch</u> him. Do you <u>see</u> her? We <u>look</u> for her. She <u>finds</u> him.

ear: We <u>hear</u> him. They <u>listen</u> to her.

heart: They <u>hate</u> him. We <u>love</u> her.

brain: I <u>recognize</u> him. Do you <u>know</u> her? He <u>understands</u> her.

5. Now the plurals of both systems can be drilled to show the many different variations.

I <u>hear</u> them.	Do you <u>know</u> them?
He <u>sends</u> them a letter.	She <u>writes</u> to them often.
We <u>hear</u> them.	We <u>watch</u> them.
I <u>speak</u> to them.	She <u>asks</u> them.

6. To test the students' grasp of the difference in pronouns within the People System, give partial sentences contrasting the verbs, but ask the students to fill in the verbs with the appropriate pronoun: <u>le</u> vs. <u>lui</u>, <u>lo</u> vs. <u>le</u>, direct vs. indirect.

I hear.	They see.	Do you hear?
She listens to.	We write.	They speak to.
He loves.	I hate.	We ask.
They answer.	She recognizes.	I lend.

These can now be drilled in the plural, and with negatives.

7. Try some short translations in English to see if the students can produce the correct answers by visualizing the verbs on the face.

We watch her.	I love him.
They know him.	She sends him cookies.
I obey her.	We recognize her.
Do you understand him?	Do you hear him?
He hates her.	They write her weekly.

8. If the concept has been grasped, and if you hear students start correcting themselves and each other by saying, "That's a mouth verb, an eye verb," you will become increasingly aware that visualizing the grammar is effective for many visually oriented students.

9. Where there are errors, point out where the verb comes from on the body. Is it a communication verb using the hand and mouth?

Once students have mastered the People System it should then be contrasted with the Thing System so that students do not make errors in reproducing "I write it," and "I write to him."

1-1 FACE

1-2 FACE (FRENCH)

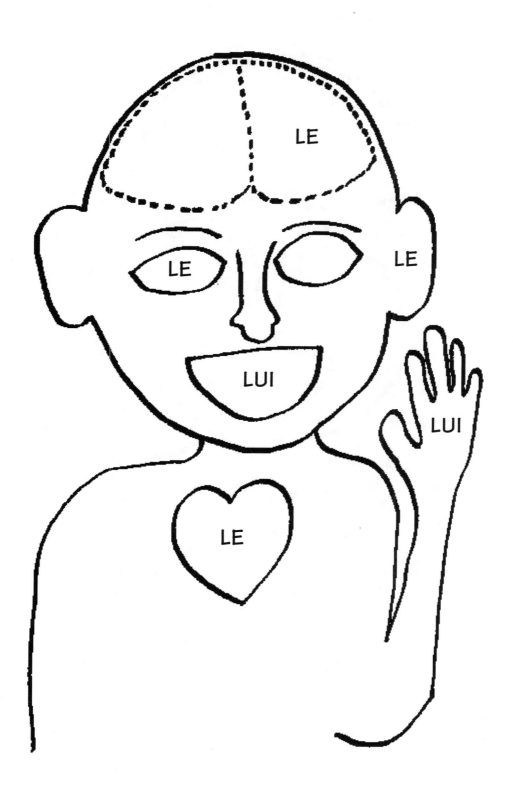

1-3 FACE (SPANISH)

ANIMAL FACES: Pronoun Placement (for Latin Languages)

Since the Latin language pronouns generally precede the verb, it is difficult to teach this concept to students who have been trained in the germanic syntax in which the pronouns follow the verb. Using the color-coded animal faces described in Step 2, the teacher can drill the basic placement of affirmative and negative statements in which direct or indirect object pronouns are used. To drill the placement, the teacher should first review meanings of the object pronouns.

HOW TO USE THE VISUAL DIAGRAM

1. Using the animal faces shown in the visual diagram, explain the point of the lesson—placing object pronouns before the verb. Then give a sample sentence such as: <u>Yo te veo</u>, or <u>Je te vois</u>.

2. Pointing out the sentence elements, the teacher places the subject pronoun in the sheep head, the object pronoun in the cow head, and the verb to the right of the cow head. Colored pens are more effective. Use different colors for each pronoun.

3. Drill some samples with the students so that the pattern is firmly established.

SPANISH	FRENCH:
Yo le doy	Je lui donne.
El me mira	Il me regarde.
Nosotros lo llamamos	Nous l'appelons.

(To the tune of the refrain from the *Lone Ranger* show, I sing, "to the left, to the left, to the left of the verb," as a reminder of the object pronoun placement.)

4. Ask other volunteers to create a verbal sentence while either you or the student points to each visual element at the board or on the overhead.

5. If students are ready for the negated version, place a big NO along the fence. Pointing to each visual element, model the negative format students should echo:

<u>YO NO TE VEO.</u>	<u>JE NE TE VOIS PAS.</u>
Yo no le doy.	Je ne lui donne pas.
El no me mira.	Il ne me regarde pas.
Nosotros no lo llamamos.	Nous ne l'appelons pas.

6. Student volunteers should follow with more examples of the negative format.

7. The student behind the volunteer could be given the job of completing the sentence with another syntactical element, such as an adverb of time.

Yo no te veo <u>ahora.</u> (Je ne te vois pas <u>maintenant</u>.)

This encourages the students to listen to one another.

8. You may want to proceed to the other pronouns to practice the different kinds of verbs. (Yo le hablo.) (Je lui parle.)

9. Continue to reinforce the differences between the direct and indirect object pronouns by using these charts. For example, call out an object pronoun such that an individual student would have to make up the rest of the sentence, pointing out each element on the chart (except the verb).

EXAMPLES:

"LE":	Student gives	"El le presta."
"LO":	Student gives	"Yo lo tengo."
"LUI":	Student gives	"Il lui prête."
"LE":	Student gives	"Je l'ai."

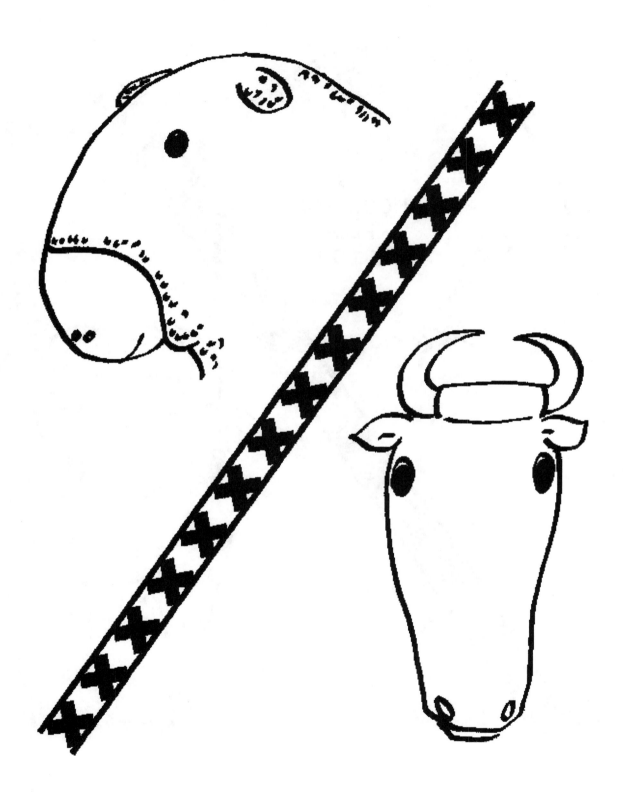

1-5 ANIMAL FACES

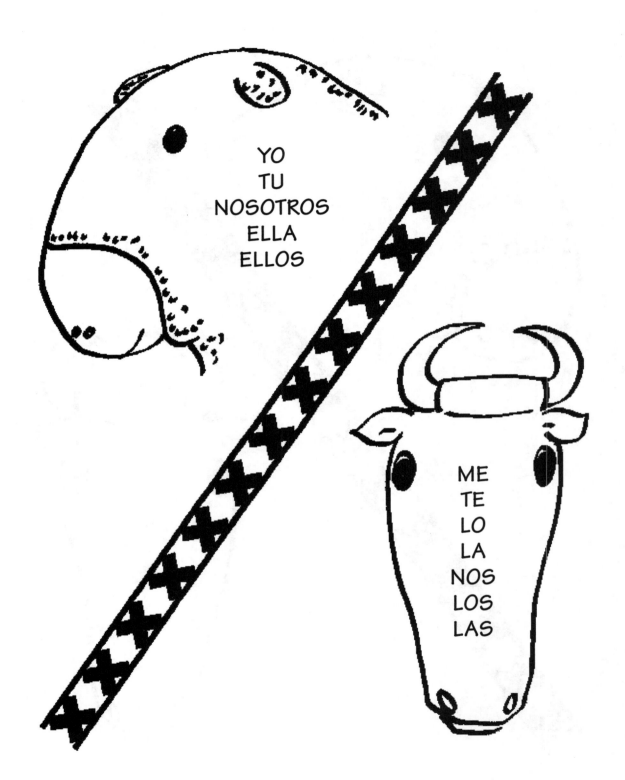

YO
TU
NOSOTROS
ELLA
ELLOS

ME
TE
LO
LA
NOS
LOS
LAS

©1996 by The Center for Applied Research in Education

12

RAINFALL / PUDDLES: Double Object Pronouns (for Spanish)

HOW TO USE THE VISUAL DIAGRAM

1. Show the single object pronouns as raindrops that combine in puddles of ME LO, TE LO, NOS LO, and SE LO, people before things, indirect before direct. Point out that LE and LES make a special combination with the other "L" words to form SE LO.

2. Drill the puddle formations with different subject and verb combinations. This can include double verbs, commands, and verbs in tenses. Also drill these with negatives. Use the following exercises. Students may volunteer added examples.

El me lo escribe.	¡Escríbamelo!
Yo te lo doy.	¡Dáselo!
¡No nos lo preste!	Yo se lo escribí.
¿Tú se lo vas a dar?	¿Vas a dárselo?
El se lo está haciendo.	El está haciéndoselo.
Yo no te lo voy a mandar.	El no me lo quiere hacer.

3. Now drill the other puddle formations of ME LA, ME LOS, and ME LAS to show the different changes in direct objects, such that the sound will not always be LO.

El me escribe la carta.	El me la escribe.
El me manda los artículos.	El me los manda.
Ella me presta las blusas.	Ella me las presta.
Tú no me das el libro tuyo.	Tú no me lo das.

4. Try the same exercise with additional combinations of TE LA, NOS LOS, SE LAS, and others.

Papá te la compra.	Papá nos los compra.
Papá se las compra.	Papá no me la compra.

5. Try some simple translations from English at this point.

He writes it for me.	He writes it for us.
She writes it for you.	She writes it for them.
She writes it for him.	He gives them to her.
Sing it to her!	Sing it to us!
Read them to her!	Read them to him!

6. Reiterate the memorization of the four basic puddles (ME LO, TE LO, NOS LO, and SE LO) just to recap the lesson.

1-6 RAINFALL/PUDDLES

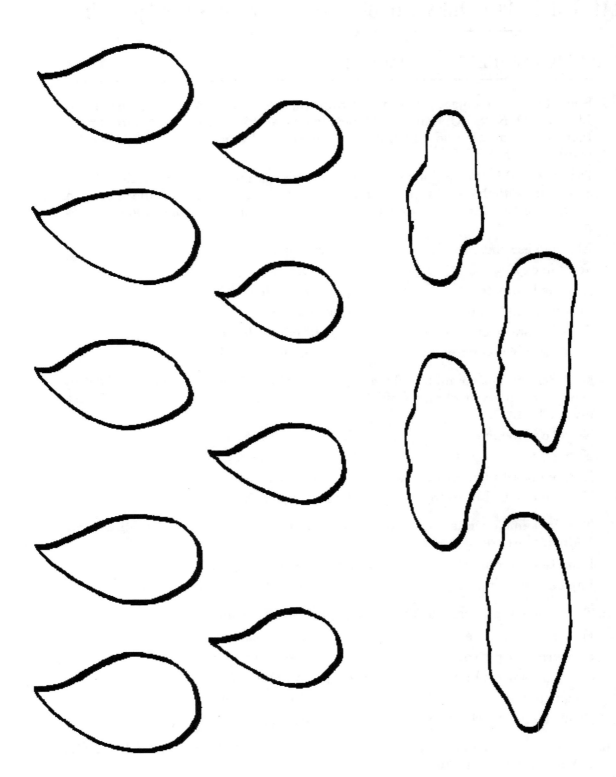

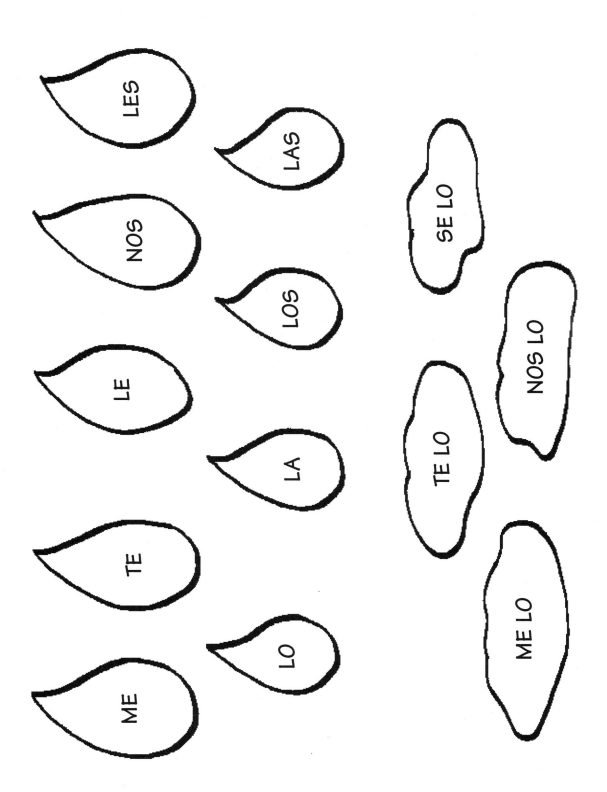

DIALOGUE CARTOONS: Using Object Pronouns

HOW TO USE THE VISUAL DIAGRAM

The left side shows the target language. The right side shows the native language. Now that the pronouns (single and double) have been studied, they can be practiced in a dialogue format on an overhead.

STEPS

1. Point to the underlined noun on the left (camisa) and ask students which pronoun combination fits the it to me (on the right).
2. Students in an advanced class may be able to provide the pronoun combination in the context of the whole dialogue. For the less advanced, provide the rest of the context before the whole class repeats it.
3. The class as a whole should repeat the entire right side as the teacher points out each section:

   Thanks.
   My friend Kathy
   gave it to me.

4. Proceed as above with the other three minidialogues.
5. Review as a class all the right side dialogues.
6. Choose students to play the parts of 1A, 1B, 2A, 2B, through 4A and 4B (all four dialogues).
7. Remove the overhead.
8. Next, read a left-sided dialogue, in mixed order (e.g., 3A, then 2A, etc.), to which the class, or individuals, respond with either memorized answers or—even better—their own creative answers.
9. Now improvise with more relevant class examples such as, "María, ¿Me prestas tu bolígrafo?" ("Maria, will you lend me your pen?")

1-9

¡ME GUSTA TU CAMISA!
THANKS! MY FRIEND KATHY GAVE IT TO ME.
ME GUSTA TU SUETER.
THANKS! MY COUSIN LENT IT TO ME. I GAVE IT AS A GIFT TO HIM LAST YEAR.

1-10

GHOST: FAIRE FAIRE—Causative Structure

The difficulty in this concept is to differentiate between the need for a direct or an indirect object pronoun.

HOW TO USE THE VISUAL DIAGRAM

1. Give some English examples of this structure and explain that it is used to express a person's making someone else do something, as in, Mom makes me study or Dad makes me mow the lawn.
2. Draw the diagram on the board of the sentence with two different ghosts, one above, one below. Place LE inside the ghost above, and LUI inside the ghost below.
3. Explain that LE (and LA), the direct object pronoun, is used when the verbal idea ends with a verb. Practice with some model sentences in French. Point to the ghost above. Use these examples:

Je le fais chanter.	Tu le fais travailler beaucoup.
Il le fait écrire.	Nous la faisons chanter.

4. Explain that LUI, the indirect object pronoun is used when the verb idea is followed by a direct object, thus extended. Practice with some model sentences in French. Point to the ghost below. Note that the hat represents the extension or addition of an object to the sentence.

Je lui fais écrire la rédaction.	Nous lui faisons chanter le refrain.
Tu lui fais laver la vaisselle?	Ils lui font lire le texte.

5. Mix and match the verbal setups such that students will repeat them but adding the LE or LUI. Where there is an error, say, "Wrong ghost."

Tu fais payer l'addition.	Je fais rire.
Il fait pleurer.	Nous faisons copier les pages.
Tu fais passer l'aspirateur.	Vous faites nettoyer la chambre.

6. Erase JE LE FAIS and JE LUI FAIS. Repeat the sentences in Step 5.
7. Try some English translations, first with LE vs. LUI, then add the other pronouns (ME, TE, NOUS, VOUS).

You make him cry.	You make him do the dishes?
I make her write the sentence.	I make her sing.
They make him pay.	They make him pay all the bills.
They make her understand.	They make her understand the reason.

   Other Variations

You make me cry.	You make them cry.

I make them write the sentence	I make them sing.
They make us pay.	They make us pay all the bills.
We make them understand.	We make them understand the reason.

8. Once the concept has been learned, experiment with other verbal variations, such as affirmative and negative commands, and passé composé. See "Apples and Orchards."

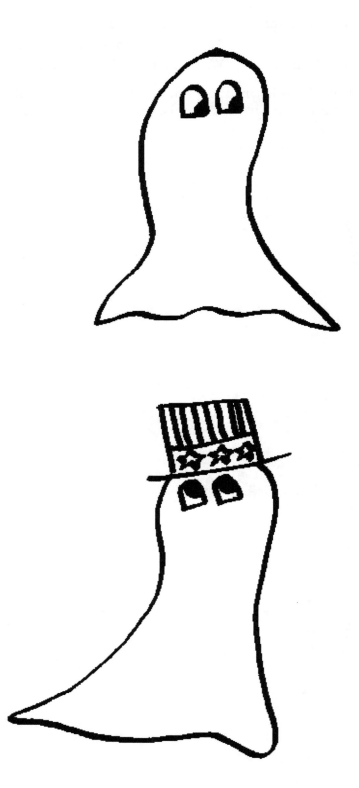

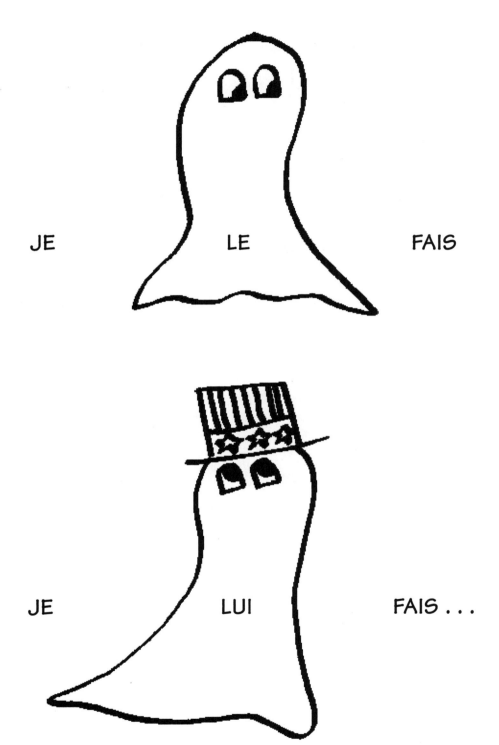

JE   LE   FAIS

JE   LUI   FAIS . . .

HOUSE: Objects of Prepositions

Prior to teaching this, the definitions of the prepositions must be taught—and learned.

HOW TO USE THE VISUAL DIAGRAM

1. Fill in the levels of the house with many different common prepositions—with the exception of CON, which will be reserved for the roof.
2. Fill in the extended rooms to the right with the objects of the preposition, as suggested.
3. Drill the common preposition-pronoun combinations as suggested in the following exercises.

para mí	detrás de ti	en ellos
sin ti	delante de nosotros	cerca de mí
para ti	lejos de ellas	detrás de nosotros

4. Now place CON in the roof with MIGO and TIGO melting into the chimneys.
5. Drill the combinations of CONMIGO and CONTIGO as contrasted with CON EL, CON ELLA, and the other combinations. Point out that in this preposition system the only exceptions to be memorized are in the roof. Explain that CON acts slightly differently from the other prepositions.

conmigo	contigo	con ella
con él	con nosotros	con usted
con ustedes	con ellos	con ellas

6. Using all the prepositions listed from the roof to the bottom of the house, elicit the forms of MI or MIGO then TI or TIGO.

para	en	con
detrás de	con	delante de
con	sin	cerca de

7. Erase the rooms of the house to the right. Have the students reproduce the pronouns in order.
8. Drill with short prepositional phrases in English.

for me	with me	behind us
far from you	for you	about you
against us	close to her	with us
in front of me	with you	without him

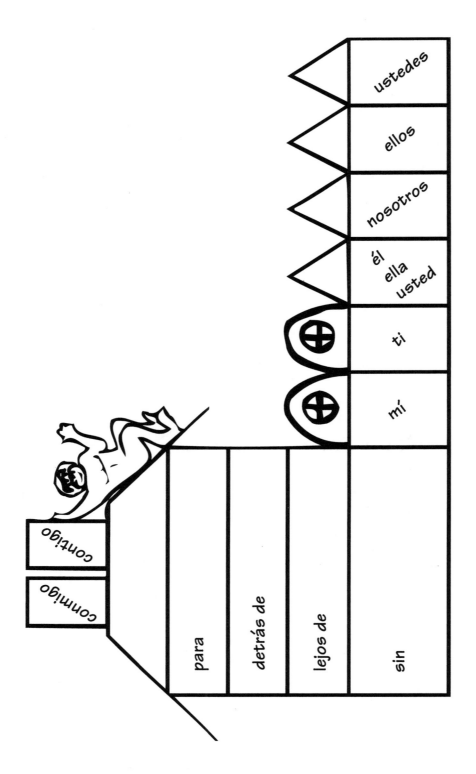

ustedes

ellos

nosotros

él
ella
usted

ti

mí

contigo

conmigo

para

detrás de

lejos de

sin

present

past

future

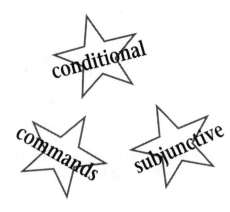

conditional

commands

subjunctive

TENSES

present perfect

imperfect

present progressive

A WORD ABOUT TENSES

In many foreign language classes, time has been taken to differentiate between tenses and moods, and to teach the conditional, the subjunctive, and the imperative, as moods rather than tenses. In keeping with a minimalist approach toward "grammar speak" to a generation of language learners who are less linguistically conscious than in previous generations, no delineation is made in this section of the difference between the two.

If you think it is appropriate to teach the difference, especially to gifted language learners, the following grammatical explanations do not preclude such an emphasis.

VERB FLASH CARDS: Present Tense of Irregular Verbs

INTRODUCTION: Teaching the present tense of verbs is an arduous task for the teacher and for the learner. Students are expected, from the very beginning of language learning, to master verb conjugations, a foreign concept in itself. It may be more prudent to have students work with verbs for a while, before they are held accountable for the appropriate endings.

Several texts introduce irregular verbs first, then the regular first conjugations, because those verbs are a natural outgrowth of the context presented. Other texts present regular conjugations at the very beginning.

The suggestion here is to present all four sentence patterns of each subject pronoun first. One statement, one interrogative, one negative, and two negatives ("No, I don't. . . .") should first be presented for "I." Once those four patterns have been mastered, the same can be presented for "you," and all subsequent pronouns. The focus is not on the pronoun, at first. It is on the sentence pattern.

One note about irregular verbs. Some verbs have difficult spellings, such as the verb venir, where the ie combination is crucial. Students often don't copy this correctly. To resolve this problem, write or type the words on the xeroxed cards so that the students will write the native language on the back. For extra spelling reinforcement, the students may be encouraged to write the target language verbs one time on the front. For example, students should copy the teacher's correct spelling: viene, venimos, and so on.

Before students drill the words themselves, pronounce each verb for them to echo.

PROCEDURE

1. Reproduce the page of verbs. Using a paper cutter, cut down the middle of the page vertically, then cut horizontally to create blocks of verbs with two sentence patterns on them.

2. Distribute the "I" verb forms. Students should have two blocks containing all four syntactical patterns. They rip the blocks to create four smaller blocks.

3. Instruct them to pick up one block, then to write the target language word on the other side. Do this for all four blocks. Point out the necessary punctuation.

4. Pronounce the words with the students, then ask the students to play solitaire with the "I" blocks. First, looking at the target language side, they should guess the meaning, flipping over the block when they correctly guess the meaning. Once all four are correct, students should look at the native language side and guess the target language side. If a mistake is made, students should redo the blocks.

5. Proceed with the "you" cards, then all the other single subject pronouns. Make sure that time is provided to play solitaire after each pronoun is covered. Students should not be overwhelmed, but rather feel that they have control over the new situation; thus, it is recommended that only the single pronouns be presented on one day. On the following day, the plural forms can be presented.

6. Students should now mix up all the single subject pronouns with the target language side up, and try a solitaire strategy to guess the new language before turning the cards over, that is, with the native language side up.

7. After solitaire, students can drill "Pick 5." Each student picks five cards in the native language and asks a partner to guess the new language. The other partner takes his or her turn. This is a good opportunity for students to listen to each other and to learn from one another.

8. Request a show of hands: How many had partners with a score of four or five? With instant feedback, you can determine whether the students comprehend the concept. If many errors are being made, request another "Pick 5."

9. The day following the initial presentation, have a review using solitaire or a "Pick 5" drill, after which the plural subject pronouns are introduced in the same manner, followed by the same drills.

10. Several pages contain English verbs for use with ESL students. These pages can also be used by Foreign Language students to write newly learned verbs on the back of each card.

Yo vengo.	¿Vengo yo?
Yo no vengo.	No, yo no vengo.
Tú vienes.	¿Vienes tú?
Tú no vienes.	No, tú no vienes.
El viene.	¿Viene él?
El no viene.	No, él no viene.

Nosotros venimos.	¿Venimos nosotros?
Nosotros no venimos.	No, nosotros no venimos.
Ustedes vienen.	¿Vienen ustedes?
Ustedes no vienen.	No, ustedes no vienen.
Ellos vienen.	¿Vienen ellos?
Ellos no vienen.	No, ellos no vienen.

Je viens.	Est-ce que je viens?
Je ne viens pas.	Non, je ne viens pas.
Tu viens.	Est-ce que tu viens?
Tu ne viens pas.	Non, tu ne viens pas.
Il vient.	Est-ce qu'il vient?
Il ne vient pas.	Non, il ne vient pas.

Nous venons.	Est-ce que nous venons?
Nous ne venons pas.	Non, nous ne venons pas.
Vous venez.	Est-ce que vous venez?
Vous ne venez pas.	Non, vous ne venez pas.
Ils viennent.	Est-ce qu'ils viennent?
Ils ne viennent pas.	Non, ils ne viennent pas.

1-15—CONTINUED

I have.	You have.
Do I have?	Do you have?
I don't have.	You don't have.
No. I don't have.	No. You don't have.

He has.	We have.
Does he have?	Do we have?
He does not have.	We do not have.
No. He does not have.	No. We do not have.

They have.	You have. (plural)
Do they have?	Do you have?
They don't have.	You don't have.
No. They don't have.	No. You don't have.

I am.	I am not.
Am I?	No, I am not.
You are.	You are not.
Are you?	No, you are not.
She is.	She is not.
Is she?	No, she is not.

He is.	He is not.
Is he?	No, he is not.
We are.	We are not.
Are we?	No, we are not.
They are.	They are not.
Are they?	No, they are not.

HAND: Verb Endings—Present Tense

INTRODUCTION: The visual hand is meant to be supported and drilled by using the real hand. This is used for verbs that have five different endings. Although it can be used for Spanish -ar, -er, and -ir verbs, this visual diagram will be used here only for the purpose of introducing -ar verbs—of introducing students to the concept of using different endings to indicate the different subjects.

PROCEDURE

1. On the overhead, or at the board, or on a real hand, assign "I" to the thumb, "you" to the index finger, "he, she, (and usted)" to the next, "we" to the fourth finger, and "they" and "you" (plural) to the last finger. Repeat this a couple of times.

2. Now, on the board or overhead, write the root of an -ar verb in the palm of the hand. Place an O on the thumb, pointing out that this represents "I." With several -AR verbs off to the side, practice some examples orally: MIRO, HABLO, GANO.

3. Place -AS on the index finger, remind the students of its meaning, then practice tú forms of the verb.

4. Proceed with all fingers on the hand, always followed by student repetition.

5. Erase the endings at the board, or on the overhead. Have the students recall all the endings, in order.

6. Have each student hold up a hand and count off with an easy verb such as mirar. As you hold the thumb, students should call out, chorally, "miro." After you point out each finger in order, the fingers should be mixed, first the index, then the ring finger, and so forth. Drill with one easy verb until no errors are heard as students call out the answers.

7. Using another verb, call on individuals to see if the majority of students can guess correctly, using a mixed order of fingers.

8. Now proceed via native language translation: I watch, they watch, we watch, and so on. Assist students by pointing to the correct finger if they hesitate. Drill until no errors are heard.

9. The following day, before homework is corrected, lead the class in a quick drill of an easy verb with the five fingers.

This is a very kinesthetic, visual presentation of verb endings, as opposed to the standard list of endings (which still has a place in summation of the concept).

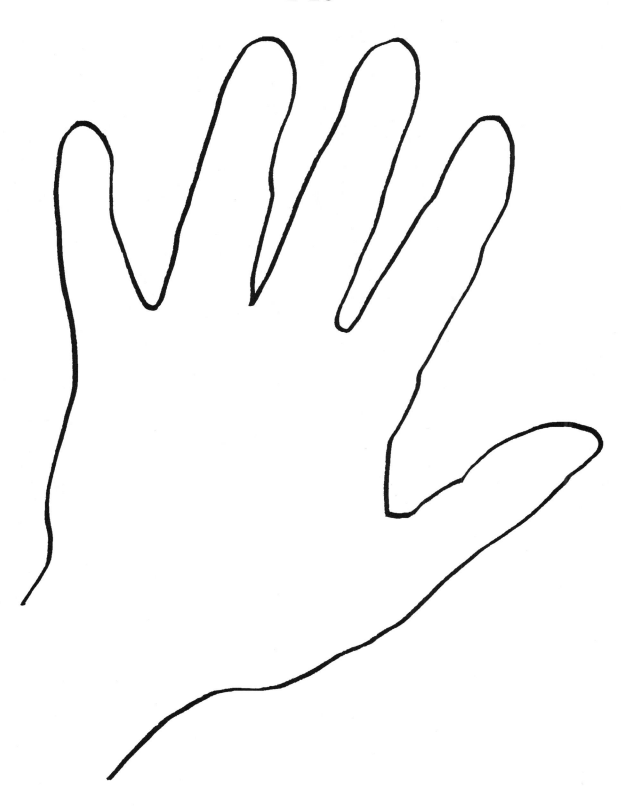

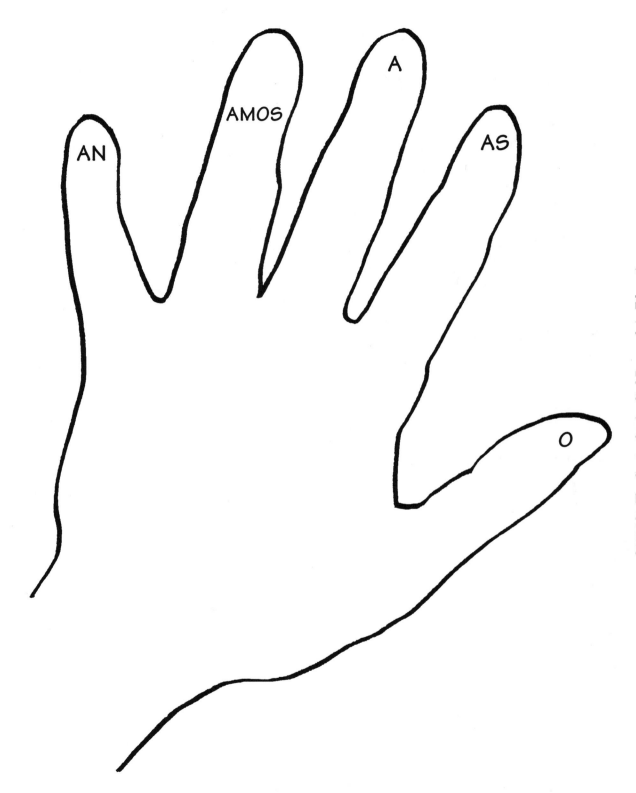

SOCKS: Stem-Changing Verbs—Spanish

PURPOSE: To show that stem changes usually occur to four subject pronouns while the fifth subject pronoun ("we") remains unchanged, like the infinitive.

INTRODUCTION: An adaptation of the "boot" or "shoe" verbs, this presentation is a learning strategy for those students who have difficulty breaking down sounds or letter combinations, then of reconstructing them.

HOW TO USE THE VISUAL DIAGRAM

1. For each verb being presented, prepare overhead transparencies or draw the two socks shown in the visual diagrams. The top stem-changing sock has five vertical sections for the verb root, and four horizontal sections for the endings. The bottom section will have four vertical root sections and only one ending section, that of <u>nosotros</u>. Name the verb and its meaning. In this instance, QUERER will be showcased.

2. Insert one letter per vertical space (Q-U-I-E-R). Then, in the first space to the right of R, enter O. Practice saying this verb form with its subject pronoun (<u>yo</u>) with the students, as follows:

   Yo quiero.   Yo no quiero.   No. Yo no quiero.

3. Insert the following endings in each box: ES, E, EN. Practice these orally with their pronouns. You may want to draw an eye to the left of the letter "I" to highlight the spelling difference between the top sock and the bottom one.

Tú quieres.	Tú no quieres.
Ella quiere.	El no quiere.
Usted quiere.	Usted no quiere.
Ellos quieren.	Ustedes no quieren.

4. Go back and review the <u>yo, tú, él,</u> and <u>ellos</u> forms by calling out the pronouns.

tú	Juanita	Pablo
usted	yo	tú y el
ustedes	ella	tú y ella

5. When students answer correctly, proceed to <u>nosotros</u> by adding EMOS to the toe of the sock and QUER in the vertical sections. Practice with the students.

Nosotros queremos.	Nosotros no queremos.
Tú y yo queremos.	Tú y yo no queremos.

6. Call out a variety of pronouns, including compound subjects, so that you can hear whether students are pronouncing the words correctly.

tú y él	tú y yo	usted y yo
él y ella	ellas	yo
tú	usted	nosotros

7. You may choose some native language translations.

I want.	He wants.	They want.
We want.	She wants.	He doesn't want.
You want.	What do you want?	

For the verb <u>Jugar</u>, the same procedure is followed, but with fewer vertical blocks. The endings represent <u>ar</u> verb endings.

For the student who has difficulty in breaking down phonological sound combinations, present the sock with the added <u>verbal</u> help of:

<u>JU</u>ice and <u>EG</u>gs & O
<u>JU</u>ice and <u>EG</u>gs & AS
<u>JU</u>ice and <u>EG</u>gs & A
<u>JU</u>ice and <u>EG</u>gs & AN
<u>JUG</u> and AMOS

Comment: While the point is shown on the socks, oral proficiency must be developed. Pronounce each form by having it then followed up by student repetition. The final step is written exercises, to see if students have mastered the difference shown by stem-changing verbs.

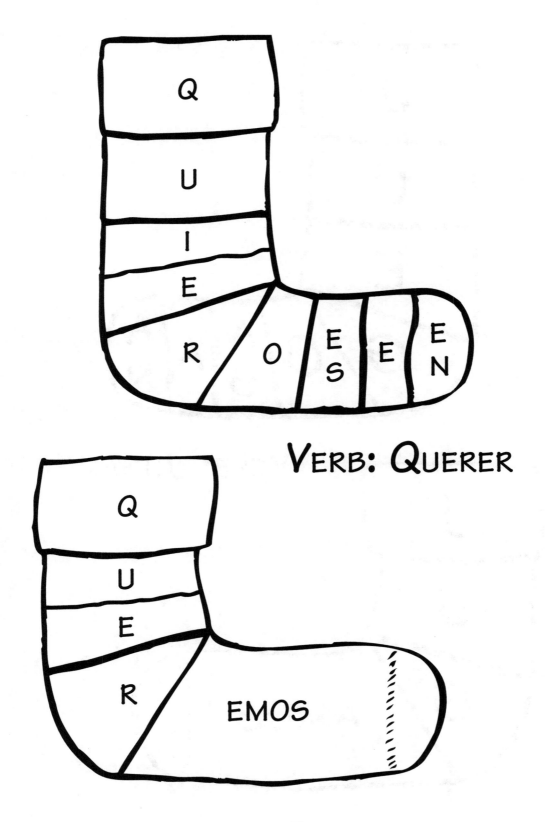

VERB: QUERER

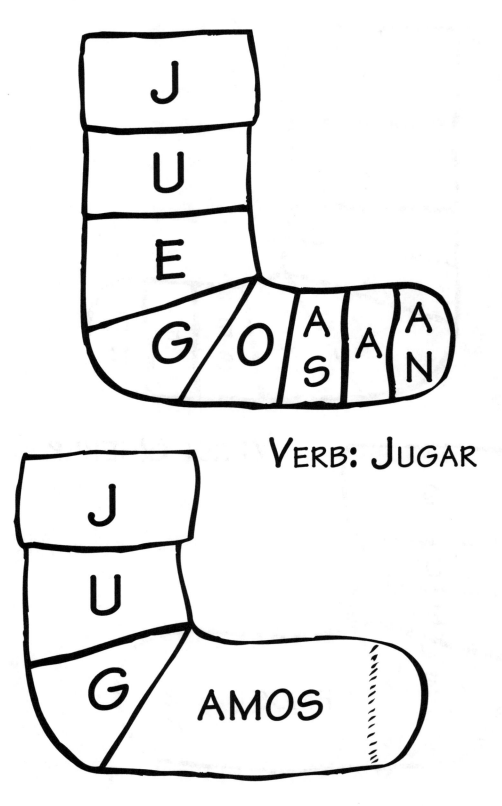

VERB: JUGAR

©1996 by The Center for Applied Research in Education

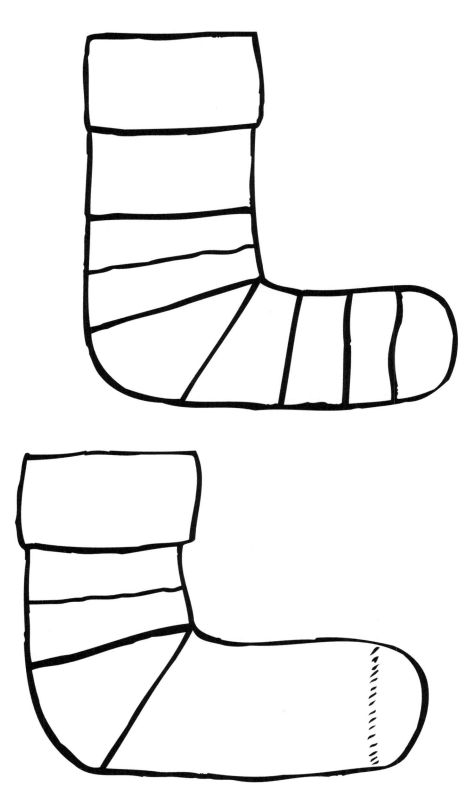

SNAKE: Commands—usted and ustedes)

Once the usted commands have been learned from the command snake, the negative tu and nosotros commands can then be taught easily. You can also teach the subjunctive forms, using the same snake image.

HOW TO USE THE VISUAL DIAGRAM

1. Explain that the command snake weaves among the three teepees.
2. Very simply explain that usted commands are formed from the yo form of the present tense and end in a "flipped vowel"—"YO plus Flip."
3. A "flipped vowel" means that all ar verbs will end in e. All er and ir will flip to a.
4. Begin at the head of the snake by placing regular ar, er, and ir verbs and drill the commands with their flipped vowels, as follows:

   Give the infinitive elicit the usted command.

   | hablar | comer | vivir |
   | cerrar | volver | pedir |

5. Move along to teepee 1 for spelling changers. Write several in the teepee and drill.

   Give the infinitive and the command form for students to repeat.

marcar: marque	pagar: pague
buscar: busque	empezar: empiece
jugar: juegue	almorzar: almuerce

6. Do the same for teepee 2 for "weird yo" forms.

   Tell students to listen to the common ga sound as they repeat after the teacher.

tener: tenga	salir: salga
venir: venga	decir: diga
poner: ponga	hacer: haga
conocer: conozca	ofrecer: ofrezca

7. Do the same for teepee 3 for the S I D E S (ser, ir, dar, estar, saber) verbs.

   Drill the infinitive and the command.

ser: sea	ir: vaya
dar: dé	estar: esté
saber: sepa	

8. Erase the verbs written on the teepees. Mix up the verbs and drill by requesting the <u>usted</u> command. It is interesting to watch how students visualize where the verb comes from. Despite the empty teepees, the students will, in their mind's eye, still see the verbs in those teepees.

GIVE	ACCEPT
dar	dé
ir	vaya
venir	venga
volver	vuelva
salir	salga
poner	ponga
vivir	viva
decir	diga
tener	tenga
pagar	pague
saber	sepa
conocer	conozca
cerrar	cierre
comer	coma
buscar	busque
ver	vea

9. Add <u>-n</u> to the end of the <u>ustedes</u> command. Mix up the verbs in Step 8 and drill by requesting the <u>ustedes</u> command.

10. At this point, you may decide to drill these verbs with the object pronouns attached.

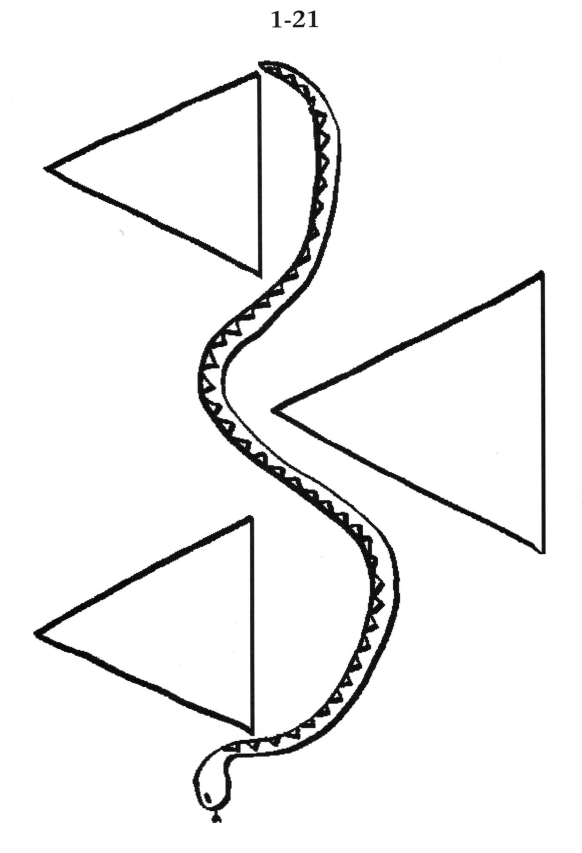

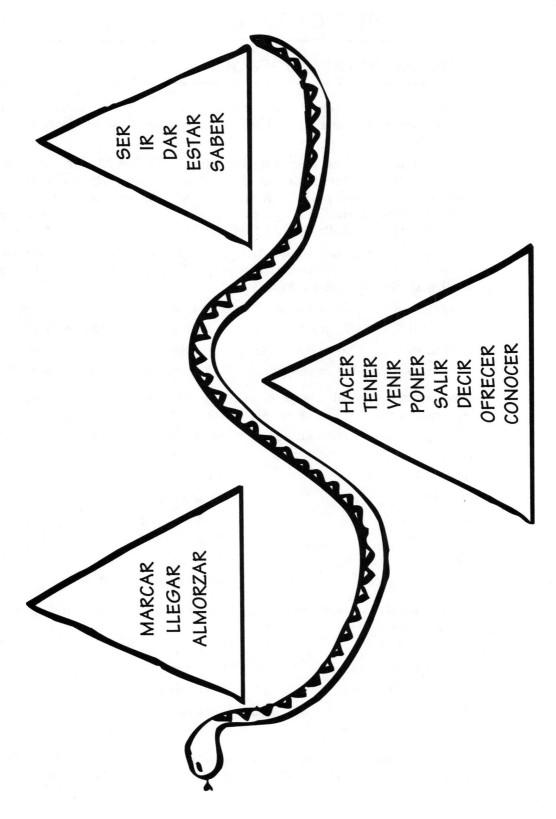

FISH AND ROD: Negative Commands

HOW TO USE THE VISUAL DIAGRAM

1. Draw fish around each pronoun attached to the right of each command or use the transparency master provided. It is important that students visualize fish around the pronouns.

2. Now explain that the preceding negatives (NO, NADA, etc.) are like fishing poles that fish each pronoun out of the water, in order. Draw simplified poles to fish the pronoun and pull it in front of the verb. As a reminder, I sing the refrain to the "Farmer in the Dell" by singing, "The NO pulls the LO, (or, the NO pulls the PRO), the NO pulls the LO, high ho the derry-o, the NO pulls the LO."

3. From the positive commands, drill the negative commands by repeating first a positive, then a negative, and by reminding students to "fish the pronoun!" Drill with the following exercises.

¡Hágalo!	¡No lo haga!	¡Dígamelo!	¡No me lo diga!
¡Ciérrela!	¡No la cierre!	¡Déselo!	¡No se lo dé!
¡Póngaselos!	¡No se los ponga!	¡Háblenos!	¡No nos hable!
¡Siéntense!	¡No se sienten!	¡Escúchelo!	¡No lo escuche!

4. Now give the students the positive command while they respond with the negative command, then vice versa. Make sure that the NO gets extra voice emphasis.

   To be given orally without seeing these on the overhead.

Give	Accept
¡Hágalo!	¡No lo haga!
¡Vístase!	¡No se vista!
¡Díganoslo!	¡No nos lo diga!
¡Hábleme!	¡No me hable!
¡Déselo!	¡No se lo dé!
¡Explíquenoslo!	¡No nos lo explique!

5. At this point, you may want to give some negative commands from English translations.

Don't do it!	Don't tell him it!
Don't speak to me!	Don't put them!
Don't write to them!	Don't answer it!
Don't close it!	Don't eat it!
Don't watch it!	Don't give it to them!

6. Recap the lesson by saying that for negative commands you "FISH IT." This is a new code word, to be used in addition to "FLIP IT!" to construct a positive command.

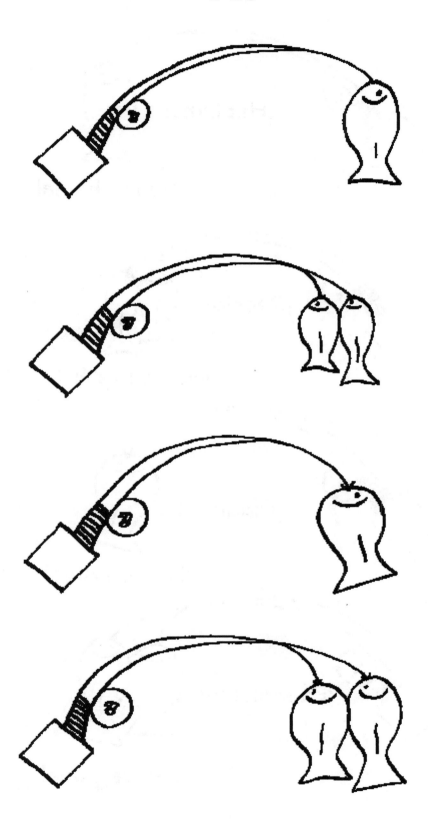

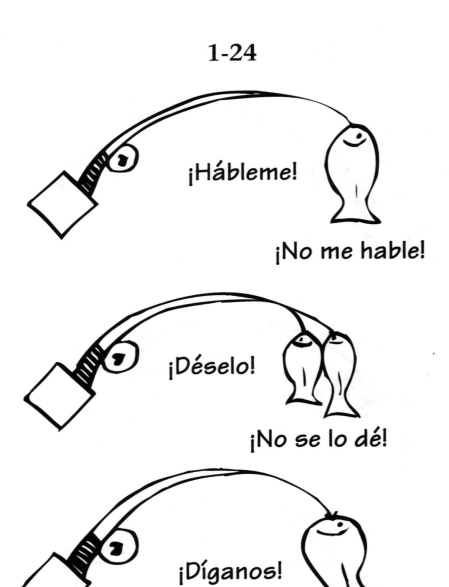

¡Hábleme!

¡No me hable!

¡Déselo!

¡No se lo dé!

¡Díganos!

¡No nos diga!

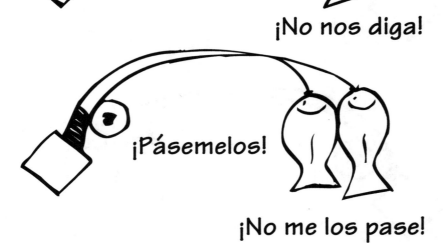

¡Pásemelos!

¡No me los pase!

TRIANGLE: Informal—Affirmative and Negative Commands for Spanish

HOW TO USE THE VISUAL DIAGRAM

1. At the corners of the inside triangle, at the board, write one example each of a <u>tú regular -ar, -er,</u> and <u>-ir</u> verb, then repeat other examples with and without pronouns. Point out "same vowel" endings or "conjugated <u>tú</u> form, minus the 's." Drill with the following:

¡Habla!	¡Come!	¡Sube!
¡Háblalo!	¡Cómelo!	¡Súbelo!
¡Juégalo!	¡Bébelos!	¡Vive!

2. Drill from the target language. (As the teacher gives the cue, the class should respond chorally.)

hablar	comer	subir
mirar	aprender	escribir
mirarlo	aprenderla	escribirlos

3. Drill from the native language.

Speak!	Eat!	Go up!
Watch!	Learn!	Write!
Watch it!	Learn it!	Write it!

4. Inside the <u>tú</u> affirmative triangle, section off three areas for <u>irregulars</u>. One section is for IR, one section for HACER and DECIR, and the other is for PONER, SALIR, TENER, VENIR, and SER. Write the infinitives first, then pointing out spelling changes and accents, and how these verbs are reduced in size (or cut), erase away the extra letters so that the new commands remain. Point out the very irregular verb <u>ir</u>.

¡Di! ¡Haz!	¡Sal! ¡Ten! ¡Pon! ¡Ven! ¡Sé!	¡Ve!
¡Dime! ¡Hazlo!	¡Ponte! ¡Tenlo!	¡Ve ahora!
¡Díselo! ¡Házmelo!	¡Ponlos! ¡Tenlos!	¡Ve allá!

5. Drill from the target language with and without pronouns.

decir, hacer	poner, salir, tener, venir, ser	ir
hacerlo, decirme	ponerlos, tenerlo	

6. Drill from the native language with and without pronouns.

Tell me! Do it!	Put it! Have it!	Go now!
Tell it to her!	Put them on!	Leave! (irse)
Do it for him!	Be nice!	

7. Contrast by drilling <u>regular</u> and <u>irregular tú</u> commands.

hablarlo	comerlo	subirlo
hacerlo	ponerlo	irse
jugarlo	beberla	ir
decírmelo	ponérselos	

8. Once it has been determined that the students grasp the <u>tú</u> affirmative commands, place the corresponding <u>usted</u> affirmative commands at the corners of the outer triangle. Along the edges, place some irregulars, such as HAGA, DIGA, VAYA, and so on.

9. Point out that the <u>tú</u> negative commands will resemble the <u>ud.</u> commands, and begin to place the negative command at the appropriate corners of the second triangle, for example, NO HABLES, NO COMAS, NO VIVAS. Along the edges, write NO HAGAS, NO DIGAS, NO VAYAS. Remind students that these forms come from the COMMAND SNAKE.

10. Drill the negative <u>tú</u> forms with and without pronouns (the same placement as in <u>ud.</u> commands). Point out the "flipped" (or opposite) vowels.

¡No hables!	¡No comas!	¡No subas!
¡No me hables!	¡No lo comas!	¡No lo subas!
¡No lo digas!	¡No lo seas!	¡No vayas!
¡No se lo hagas!	¡No te los pongas!	¡No te vayas!

11. Drill from the target language.

No, hablar	No, comer	No, subir
No, hablarme	No, comerlo	No, subirlo
No, decir	No, venir	No, ir
No, decírmelo	No, ponérselo	No, irse

12. Drill from the native language.

Don't speak it!	Don't eat it!	Don't write it!
Don't do it!	Don't put them!	Don't go there!
Don't tell me!	Don't be silly!	Don't leave!
Don't watch it!	Don't drink them!	Don't write them for her!

13. Summarize by pointing out and repeating the <u>tú</u> affirmative, then the <u>tú</u> negative, then the <u>ud.</u> positive of each corner or side of the triangle. Students should repeat after you.

¡Háblame!	¡No me hables!	¡No me hable!
¡Cómelo!	¡No lo comas!	¡No lo coma!
¡Escríbemelo!	¡No me lo escribas!	¡No me lo escriba!

| ¡Hazlo! | ¡No lo hagas! | ¡No lo haga! |
| ¡Sábelo! | ¡No lo sepas! | ¡No lo sepa! |

14. Begin this exercise with the first student in class. Assign to student 1 the job of TU+, to student 2 the job of TU-, and to student 3 the job of UD. Repeat as above for the rest of the class.

15. Now provide a verb to be passed along the line from student 1 through student 3. Repeat this until the whole class has performed. Student 4 begins the next verb.

    (TU+ to TU- to UD.)

    hablar, hablarlo, beber, beberlo, escribirlos, venir, ponerse, irse, saberlo

16. As an alternative to Step 15, you may choose to use the Command Window to continue the drill. Request from student 1 the verb from the TU+ box. Student 2 provides the UD. + form. Student 3 provides the UD.- form. Student 4 provides the TU- form. This will allow for review. It can also be expanded, at the bottom of the window, to include ustedes and nosotros commands, if desired. This alternative requires pronouns along with the verbs.

    buscarlo, comerlo, escribírmelos, ponerse, irse, saberlos

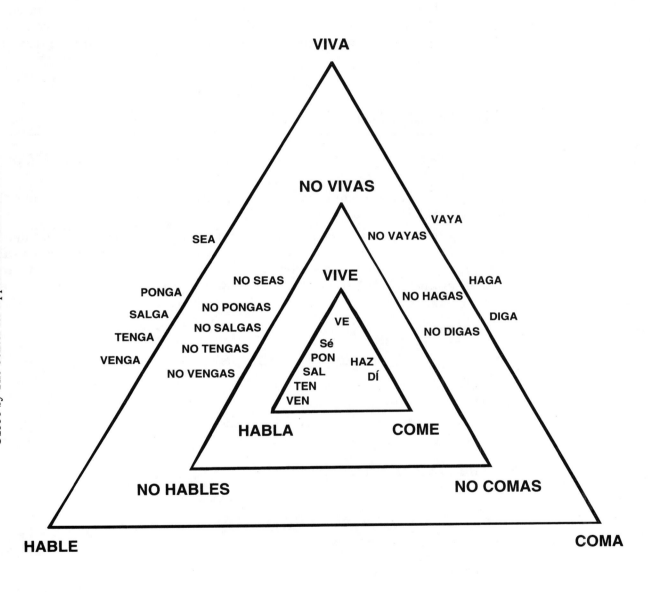

COMMAND WINDOWS: Command and Pronoun Drill

PURPOSE: A quick review of affirmative and negative commands with pronouns attached

INTRODUCTION: Once students have been exposed to both the familiar and formal commands, they may become confused not only by the different forms, but also by where the pronouns are placed. The window panes give them a reference point.

HOW TO USE THE VISUAL DIAGRAM

1. Review the social situations that would dictate the use of formal or informal commands.
2. Mark the four window panes as in the diagram and point out to the students which commands belong in which window pane.
3. Beginning in the top left, the affirmative informal (TU +) pane, give students an -ar verb with a pronoun, then ask a volunteer to give the command. Students may need to be reminded of how to form this command (conjugated tu form, minus the "s," thus, the same vowel as the infinitive, for the most part).

EXAMPLES:

GIVE	ACCEPT
hablarlo	¡Háblalo!
mirarlo	¡Míralo!
dármelo	¡Dámelo!

Proceed with -Er and -Ir verbs.

EXAMPLES:

comerlo	¡Cómelo!
subirlo	¡Súbelo!

Proceed with reflexive verbs.

EXAMPLES:

GIVE	ACCEPT
acostarse	¡Acuéstate!
despertarse	¡Despiértate!
vestirse	¡Vístete!

4. Point out the bottom left box into which will be placed the affirmative formal commands (USTED +). Proceed with the same verbs as in the examples for TU +, but remind students of the derivation of this form (<u>yo</u> form with the opposite vowel).

EXAMPLES OF -AR VERBS:

GIVE	ACCEPT
hablarlo	¡Háblelo!
mirarlo	¡Mírelo!
dármelo	¡Démelo!

EXAMPLES OF -ER AND -IR VERBS:

comerlo	¡Cómalo!
subirlo	¡Súbalo!

EXAMPLES OF REFLEXIVE VERBS:

acostarse	¡Acuéstese!
despertarse	¡Despiértese!
vestirse	¡Vístase!

5. Point out the bottom right box into which the negative formal commands (USTED -) will be placed. Remind students of the change in position of the pronoun. Then begin drilling with the same verbs as in Step 4.

EXAMPLES OF ALL VERBS:

GIVE	ACCEPT
hablarlo	¡No lo hable!
mirarlo	¡No lo mire!
dármelo	¡No me lo dé!
comerlo	¡No lo coma!
subirlo	¡No lo suba!
acostarse	¡No se acueste!
despertarse	¡No se despierte!
vestirse	¡No se vista!

6. Point out the top right window pane into which the negative informal commands (TU -) will be placed. Before asking for volunteers, remind students how to form this (the TU subjunctive form, or the USTED command form with an "s"). Using the same verbs, proceed as before.

EXAMPLES:

GIVE	ACCEPT
hablarlo	¡No lo hables!
mirarlo	¡No lo mires!
dármelo	¡No me lo des!
comerlo	¡No lo comas!
subirlo	¡No lo subas!
acostarse	¡No te acuestes!
despertarse	¡No te despiertes!
vestirse	¡No te vistas!

7. Now take any new verb, a verb not used in the drills, announce it to the class, point out the counter clockwise pattern of the TU+ pane, then the USTED+, the USTED -, then the TU- panes as the class orally gives the forms.

    You may want to use some irregular forms at this point. Students will be better able to concentrate on the irregular forms now that they have mastered the initial rules of the drill, and the grammatical changes.

    To reinforce the use of the affirmative and negative formal commands in the plural, extend the boxes at the bottom to include: USTEDES + and UST-EDES -. Start by using the verbs initially used in the drill.

EXAMPLES:

GIVE		ACCEPT
hablarlo	¡Háblenlo!	¡No lo hablen!
comerlo	¡Cómanlo!	¡No lo coman!
vestirse	¡Vístanse!	¡No se vistan!

1 | **4**

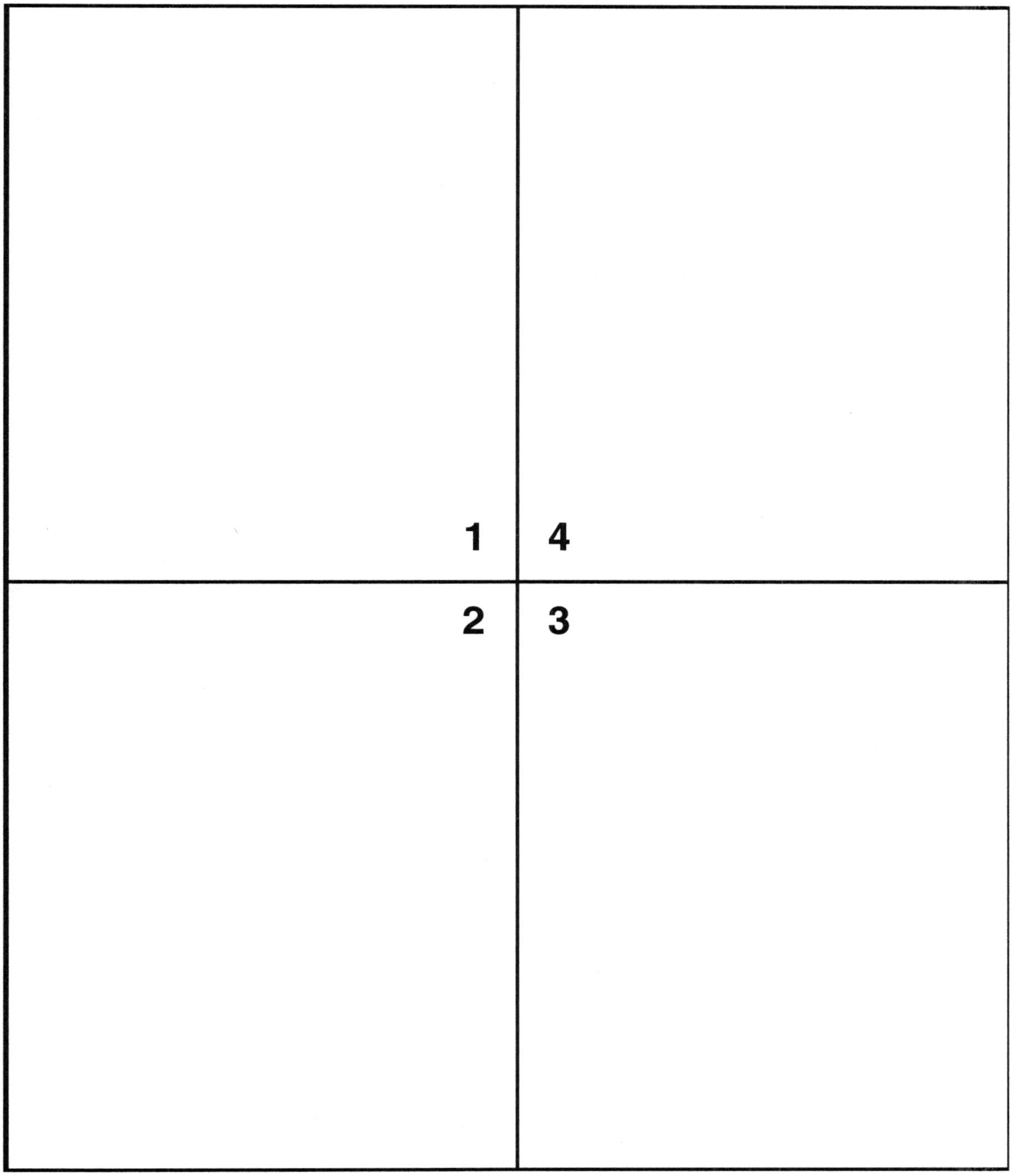

2 | **3**

TU +	**TU -**
1	**4**
2	**3**
USTED +	**USTED -**

SWEET TRIP: Command Drill with Regular and Irregular Verbs

PURPOSE: To review and reinforce the command forms of regular and irregular verbs, with pronouns attached

HOW TO USE THE VISUAL DIAGRAM

1. Explain to students that the goal is to see who can successfully arrive at the ice cream store by showing mastery of all related concepts of pronouns (direct, indirect, reflexive).

2. To keep the drill running, don't start with a student who would probably guess everything correctly.

3. With the first student in the row, ask how to express in the target language the sentence in box 1 of the path (COMERLO). Specify which commands are requested, formal, or informal.

4. If the student guesses correctly, the student may proceed to box 2. If the student misses, write the student's initials at home base.

5. If the student misses at box 3, write the student's initials next to box 2.

6. When the student misses, the next student in the row enunciates the sentence, and proceeds as indicated above.

7. Continue until someone has reached the ice cream store. As a possible reward to the student, a sticker with a colored ice cream cone may be awarded. In the meantime, the class has probably been extremely attentive to the correct answers given—and to the wrong ones, so as not to repeat the errors.

8. This drill may be done using the target language solely, or the native language through translation.

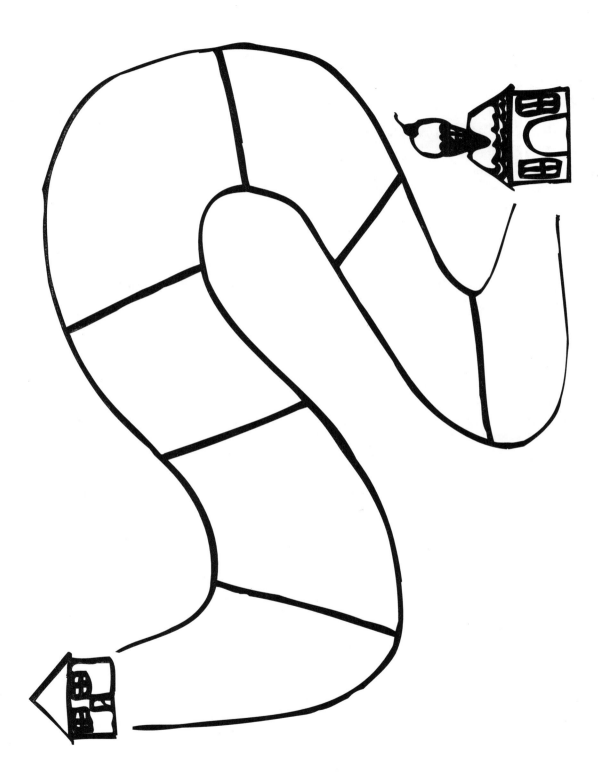

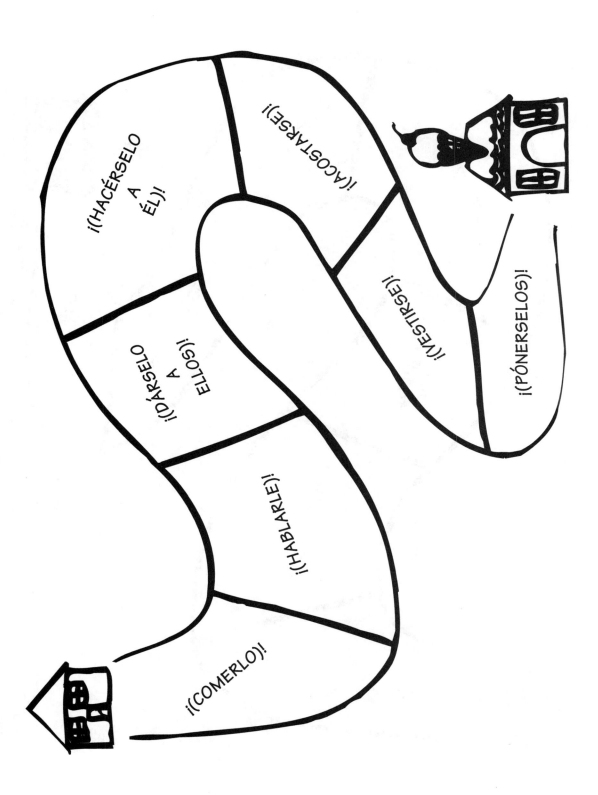

¡(HACÉRSELO A ÉL)!

¡(ACOSTARSE)!

¡(VESTIRSE)!

¡(PÓNERSELOS)!

¡(DÁRSELO A ELLOS)!

¡(HABLARLE)!

¡(COMERLO)!

1-31

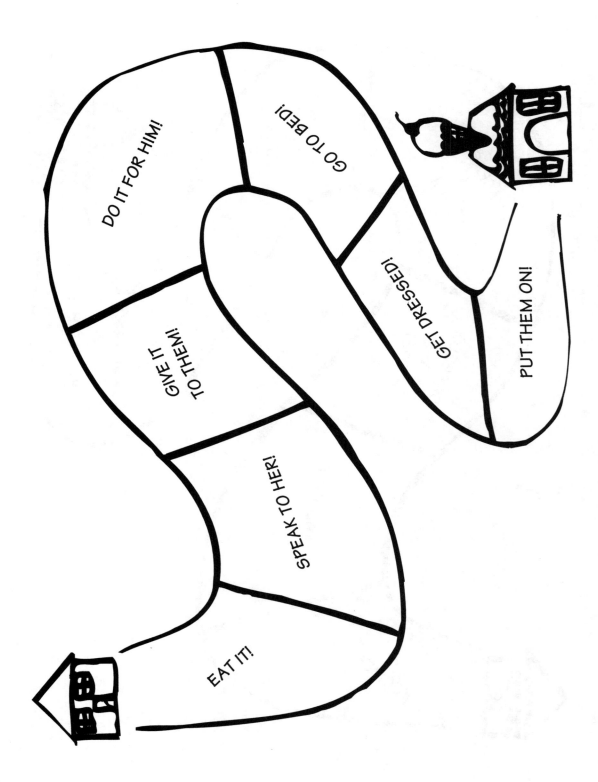

TREE (HABER TREE): Present Perfect Tense

HOW TO USE THE VISUAL DIAGRAM

1. Name the tense and give a few examples in English so that the meaning can be established.

2. Draw in the roots with the forms indicated on the diagram and practice the pronunciation with the students of: <u>yo he</u>, <u>tú has</u>, <u>él ha</u>, <u>nosotros hemos, ellos han.</u>

3. Now add ADO to the branch as you explain that these are the endings for <u>ar</u> verbs. Give some examples from infinitives. Drill using the exercises in the steps of the activities in this text. Actually move your finger from the roots to the branch as you drill each verb.

     First give some examples from the infinitive: pensar/pensado, hablar/hablado, jugar/jugado

   Now move your finger from roots to branches as students repeat:

yo he hablado	tú has cerrado	ella ha nadado
nosotros hemos jugado	ellos han buscado	ustedes han dado

4. Now add IDO to the branch as you explain that these are the endings for <u>er</u> and <u>ir</u> verbs. Give some examples from infinitives. Drill, using the suggested exercises in this text. Remember to move your finger physically from the roots to the branches.

     First give examples from the infinitive: comer/comido, beber/bebido, vivir/vivido

   Now move from the roots to the branches as students watch and repeat:

yo he vivido	tú has salido	él ha oído
nosotros hemos bebido	ellos han comido	ustedes han ido

5. Give some subjects and infinitives of <u>ar, er,</u> and <u>ir</u> verbs to drill whether students have grasped the initial steps.

yo/beber	nosotros/oír	ella/escuchar
tú/llamar	él/jugar	ellos/dar

6. Now explain that the exceptions will be placed on the TO and CHO branches at the top. As you give the infinitives of the verbs, place their TO forms (ABIERTO, ESCRITO, MUERTO, PUESTO, ROTO, VISTO, VUELTO) on the branch, and drill.

7. Do the same for the CHO forms (DICHO, HECHO).

8. Mix TO and CHO verbs and drill by giving the subject and infinitive.

yo/abrir	ella/ver	tú/escribir

| él/hacer | tú/decir | nosotros/volver |
| ella/morir | yo/romper | ella/poner |

9. Now mix all four branches.

nosotros/vivir	nosotros/ver	nosotros/volver
tú/decir	tú/dar	tú/decidir
yo/poner	yo/pensar	yo/patinar
ella/saber	ella/salir	ella/ser
ellos/hace	ellos/jugar	ellos/escribir

10. A short exercise from English translation can be used at this point.

I have written.	Have you seen?	We have watched.
They have won.	He has put.	They have played.
She has done.	I have not broken.	You have said.

You may want to include some pronouns so that correct placement of them is reinforced.

Recommendation: Repeat this drill by having students say the verbs with a pronoun, in particular, the pronoun lo.

ADO

TO

CHO

IDO

YO HE

TU HAS

ÉL HA

NOSOTROS HEMOS

ELLOS HAN

FISH FILET: Verb Tenses and Irregular Verb Forms

Prior to using this diagram, teach the verb tense or the irregular verb forms. Then use this visual diagram as a drill the day following the presentation or before a quiz.

HOW TO USE THE VISUAL DIAGRAM

(Note the Corresponding Exercises)

A. For row drills each row needs a fish.

1. Before class starts, sketch the fish on the board or use the overhead transparency. All top bones should be completed. The visual diagram merely gives suggestions. The number of bones could correspond to the number of students per row or per team.

2. On the top bones of each fish, a subject and verb infinitive of an irregular verb should be placed. An alternative would be to place the present tense on the top bones and request that the past tense be produced on the bottom.

3. When the students arrive in class, the first person in each row should write the correct verb form on the bone below the infinitive. The second student in each row should write the second form. Continue until each student has contributed.

4. To correct the students' work, ask the class which bones need to be erased because of errors. The goal is to see how many complete fish are left. Which rows have produced complete fish? Request the correct forms of the verbs from the students.

5. The next day, these fish should be recreated on the board until more and more rows produce complete fish. Ask the students to keep a tally of how many complete fish they produce from day to day. This keeps them goal oriented.

B. For a class competition of side against side, two fish must to be reproduced on the board.

1. You can either sketch on the board one fish for each side of the room or produce two fish by using two overhead machines. It is suggested that two different colors be used, for example, a blue overhead and a red one.

2. Write on the top bones either the subject and infinitive of the irregular verb or the present tense of the verbs to be studied so as to elicit the past tense.

3. Each student must fill in a bottom bone with the correct answer. The rules are flexible. Students may be obligated to fill in the next bone in line or choose to fill in a verb with which they are comfortable. Once answers are placed on the bone, only you may erase them.

4. As in the previous example, erase the incorrect answers (and bones) in response to what the students discover. This engages the attention, especially of the opponents. Again the goal is to determine which side has the most complete fish.

5. The drill should be done several days in a row until the students see that they are improving. Try for 100 percent mastery.

CORRESPONDING EXERCISES

The following are suggested as possible uses of the visual diagram for drill purposes:

French Irregular Verbs: Present Tense

Fish 1

| je/dire | il/lire | nous/connaître | vous/savoir | ils/faire |

Fish 2

| je/faire | tu/lire | nous/faire | vous/dire | elles/connaître |

French: Present to Past Tense: A drill to see if students remember the correct auxiliary verb of AVOIR or ETRE.

Fish 1

| je vais | tu fais | il voit | nous sommes | ils se lèvent |

Fish 2

| j'arrive | tu pars | elle dit | vous descendez | elles ont |

Spanish Stem-Changing Verbs: Present Tense

Fish 1

| yo/pedir | tú/decir | ella/repetir | nosotros/pedir | ellos/seguir |

Fish 2

| yo/decir | tú/pedir | él/seguir | nosotros/decir | ellas/servir |

Spanish Stem-Changing Verbs: Present to Preterit Tense

Fish 1

| pido | repites | dice | seguimos | sirven |

Fish 2

| digo | sirves | sigue | pedimos | repiten |

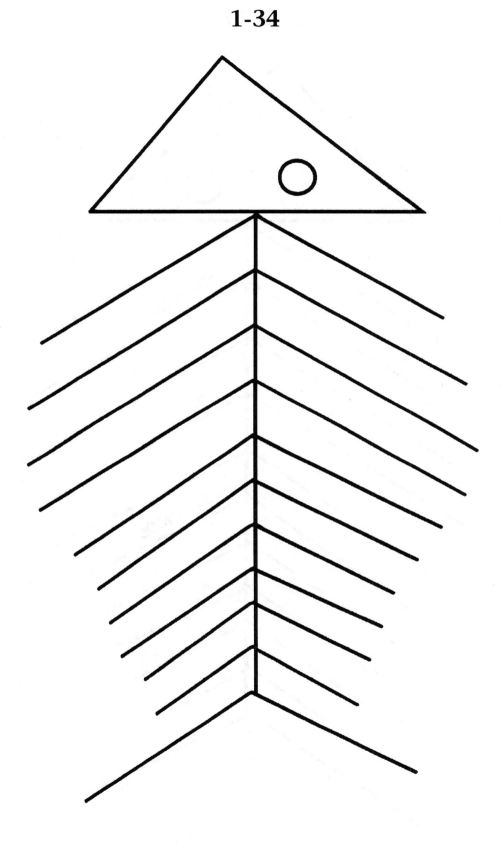

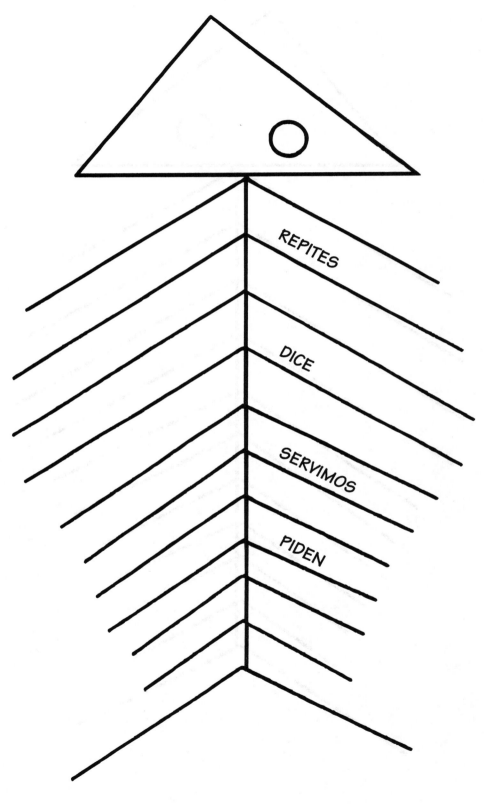

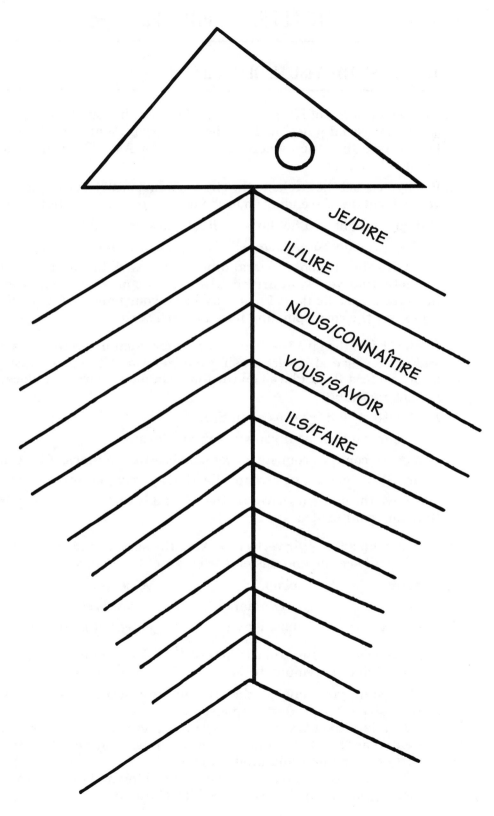

JE/DIRE

IL/LIRE

NOUS/CONNAÎTIRE

VOUS/SAVOIR

ILS/FAIRE

HOTELS: Preterit / Past Tense

HOW TO USE THE VISUAL DIAGRAM

1. In the penthouse of HOTEL A place the é, on the fourth floor <u>aste</u>, or the third ó, on the second <u>amos</u>, and on the first <u>aron</u>. Point out where Amos and his friend Aron live, then where Aste (short for Astrid?) lives. This personalizes the hotel concept.

2. Briefly instruct the students that these endings will be placed onto the <u>stem</u> of <u>ar</u> verbs. Point out the ending on each floor as you drill the endings for all <u>ar</u> verbs.

   <u>Hablar</u>: yo hablé, tú hablaste, él habló, nosotros hablamos, ellos hablaron

   <u>Nadar</u>: yo nadé, tú nadaste, ella nadó, nosotros nadamos, ellas nadaron

   Give the students several other <u>ar</u> verbs while you point out the floor of the hotel that you want drilled. The students must associate the preterit ending with a specific floor. Physically move your hand or finger up and down to represent the corresponding floor for each verb.

3. In HOTEL B (or give the hotels names for greater interest) place the preterit endings for <u>er</u> and <u>ir</u> verbs, using the <u>yo</u> form in the penthouse. <u>Ellos</u> should be on the first floor. Place <u>í</u> on the top floor, move down and place in this order: <u>iste, ió, imos, ieron.</u>

4. Drill with <u>er</u> and <u>ir</u> verbs as in Step 2.

   Point out the floor as if you were in an elevator.

   <u>Comer</u>: yo comí, tú comiste, él comió, nosotros comimos, ellos comieron

   <u>Vivir</u>: ellos vivieron, tú viviste, ella vivió, yo viví, nosotros vivimos

   Give the students several other <u>er</u> and <u>ir</u> verbs while you point to the floor that you want drilled.

5. Now mix up <u>ar</u> vs. <u>er/ir</u> verbs by asking the subject and infinitive; the students should still see the endings on each floor of the hotels.

tú/marcar	él/abrir	yo/beber
ellos/comer	yo/llamar	nosotros/salir
yo/conocer	usted/vivir	ustedes/tomar

6. Erase the verb endings in the hotels. Now drill again by mixing up the verbs. Do choral and individual drills.

7. At this point, you may ask the students to insert a direct object pronoun (<u>lo</u>) as they give their preterit responses.

   At a later point, when the irregular preterits are taught, they can be presented as "hotel jumpers." Again, you must point out how they jump from <u>e</u> to <u>iste</u> to <u>o</u> to <u>imos</u>, and finally, to <u>ieron</u>.

   The hotel concept can be used for teaching and drilling the past tense of French (<u>avoir</u> vs. <u>être</u> hotels) as well as German (<u>haben</u> vs. <u>sein</u> hotels).

A.

B.

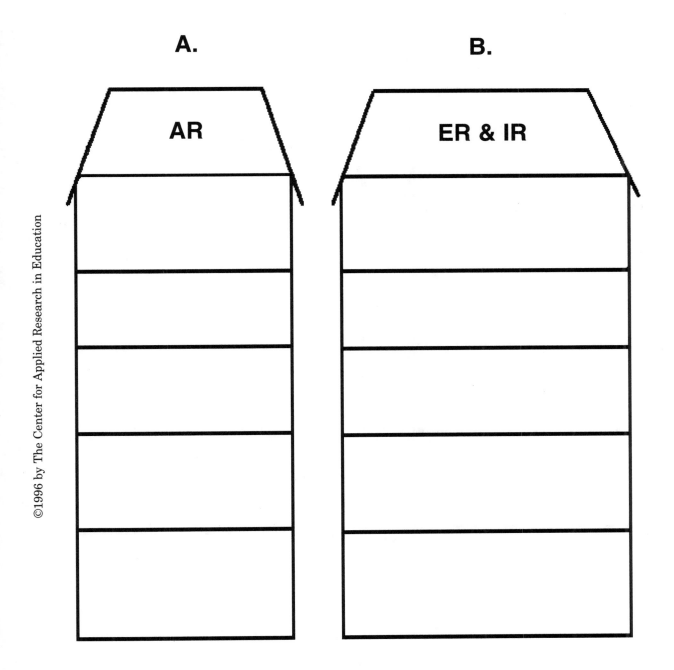

AR

ER & IR

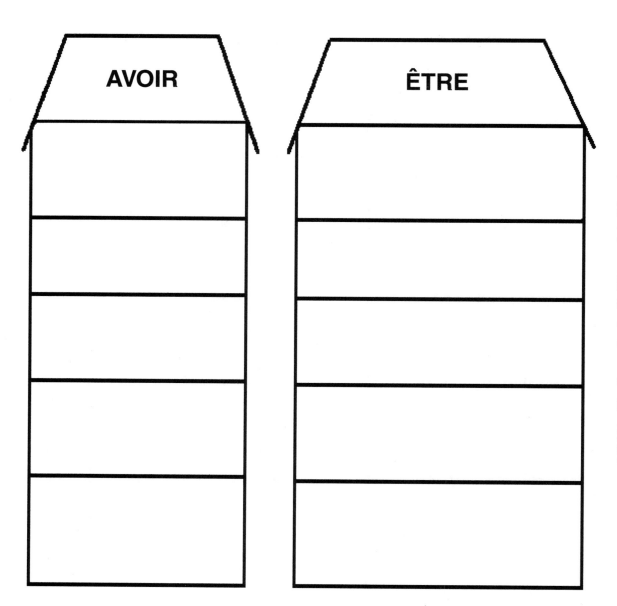

DRILL SQUARES: Past Tense

PURPOSE: To drill the forms of the past tense to which the students have already been exposed, that is, the regular and some irregular forms

HOW TO USE THE VISUAL DIAGRAM

1. Draw the boxes on the board, or use an overhead transparency. Drawing these boxes with indelible ink on an overhead enables the teacher to reuse the boxes, provided that the verbs are written in erasable ink.

2. In the center, draw the word that corresponds to the past tense (i.e., le passé composé, el préterito, etc.)

3. On the outer lines, draw the regular verbs while the inner lines should contain some irregular verbs.

4. At the corners, starting with the top left and going counterclockwise, place the subject pronouns: I, he/she, we, they. In the middle, between I and he/she, the teacher may place "you," and the plural version thereof, across from the singular.

5. Begin the drill by pointing to any corner or any line. For example, in the diagram, you might point out "el, ir." The students would then respond with "él fue."

6. After many choral drills, continue by testing individual students.

7. For variety, you may choose to place a verbal idea on the lines, rather than just the verb. Examples of this would be "to speak well," " to eat a lot," "to see an accident."

1-39

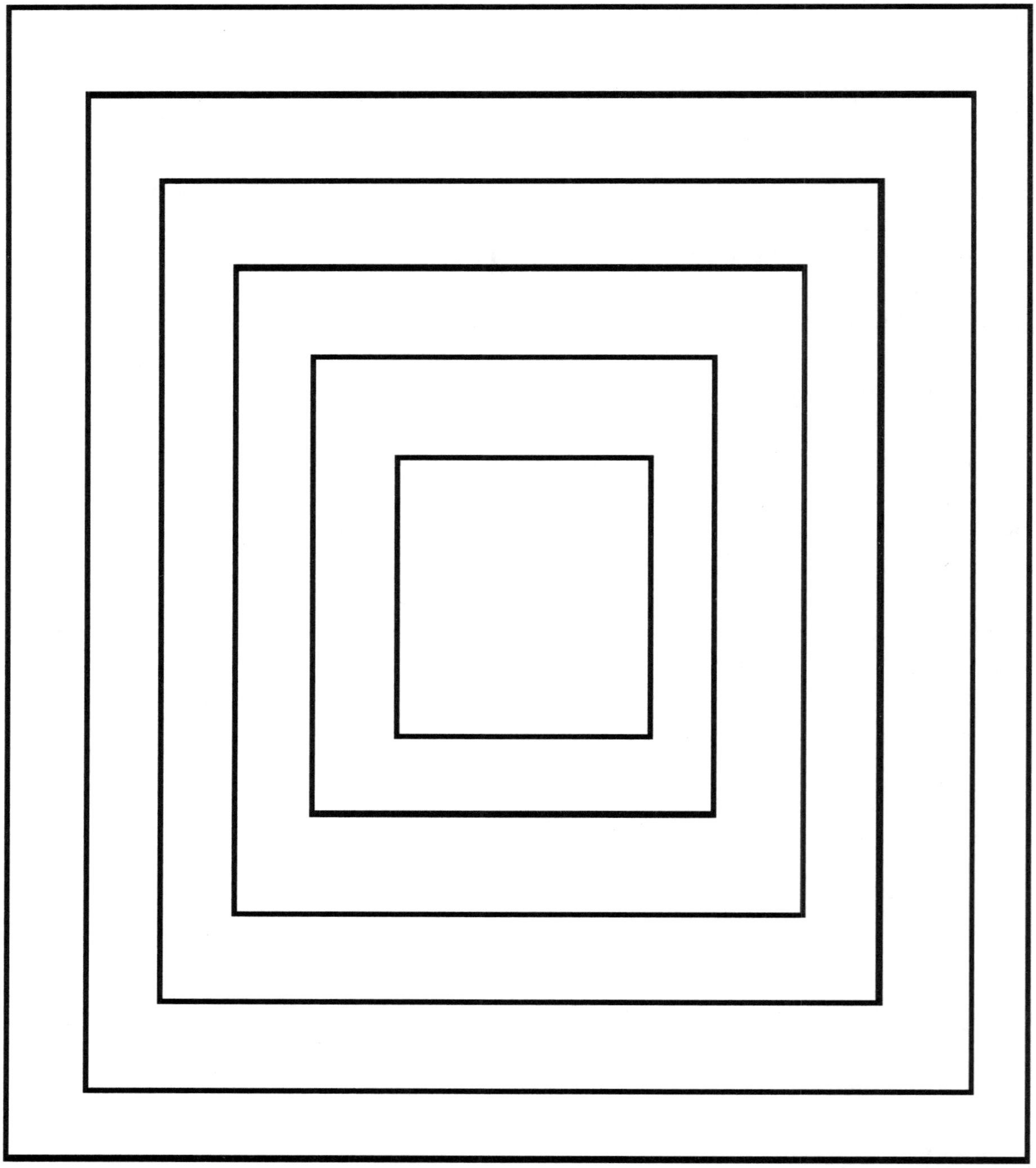

1-40

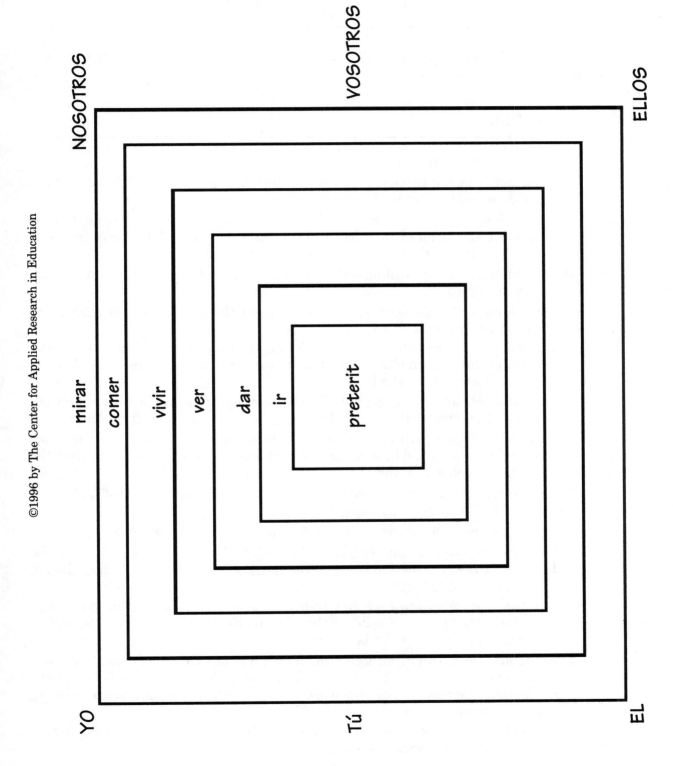

83

LETTER "L": Spanish—Preterit Spelling Changes (for -car, -gar, -zar verbs)

PURPOSE: To isolate the spelling changes of the yo form of the preterit as compared to the other subject pronouns

PROCEDURE

1. Review preterit -ar endings with a simple verb, such as mirar.
2. Point out that the three types of -ar verbs (-car, -gar, -zar) will have spelling changes in yo, but not in the other subject pronouns.
3. On the board, place a large L to illustrate the -car verbs. Along the vertical side, place the letters P E S. Then place the yo ending (QUE) above the horizontal line. Below that line, print the other endings.
4. Drill at the board by calling out different subject pronouns: ella, Juan yo, los chicos, tú, usted.
5. Have a student volunteer try another verb at the board, such as marcar, or sacar on the letter L.
6. Repeat the process with -gar verbs. For jugar, place JU going down the vertical side of the L, then GUE along and above the horizontal line of the L, then the other forms below the line.
7. Drill at the board by calling out different subject pronouns, while a volunteer tries another verb at the board. Try pegar, or llegar in the L formation.
8. Repeat the process with -zar verbs: For almorzar, place ALMOR going down the vertical side of the L, then CE above the horizontal line of the L, then the other forms below the line.
9. Drill at the board as before, while a volunteer tries another verb of its kind at the board. Try alzar or empezar.
10. Now it's time for a row drill. Place one L per row on the blackboard.
11. Give each row a -car, -gar,- or -zar verb, or place the root of each verb along the L for each row for the following verbs: buscar, marcar, pagar, pegar, llegar, alzar, comenzar, empezar, and so on.
12. Ask the first person in each row to print the yo ending along the horizontal line, the second person should do the tú form, the third should do ella, and so on, until all pronouns have been covered.
13. Stand at each L, call attention to the forms, and ask the class to evaluate how many correct answers are represented by each L. When you ask for students' evaluative responses, they are more engaged in comparing and contrasting right and wrong answers.
14. The following day of class, use this quick technique as a short warmup activity, before the homework is corrected.

1-41

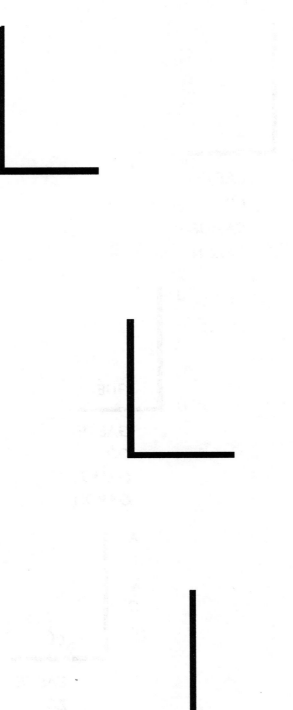

1-42

S

A QUÉ

CASTE
CÓ
CAMOS
CARON

J

U *GUÉ*

GASTE
GÓ
GAMOS
GARON

A
L
M
O
R *CÉ*

ZASTE
ZÓ
ZAMOS
ZARON

BASEMENT BOYS: Spanish—Preterit Third Person Spelling Changes

PURPOSE: To highlight Spanish preterit spelling changes in third person singular and plural

INTRODUCTION: Several kinds of verbs change the root or the ending spelling in the third person singular and plural. The concept must be learned effectively because other tenses, such as the progressive and imperfect subjunctive, are formed from this change.

HOW TO USE THE VISUAL DIAGRAM

1. Make a list of the types of affected -er and -ir verbs. For example, one might list:

A	B	C
pedir	dormir	leer
vestir	morir	oír
servir		construir

2. Beginning with one group of verbs, such as group A, explain briefly that for sound balance, the third person singular and plural verb forms will change.

3. Now show on the house, the whole yo and tu forms on each of the two levels, then the el form in the basement. Proceed to the plural side and write the preterits. Pause before entering the third person plural to focus student attention to that area, and form. State that these changes occur in the "basement" of the verb house.

4. A volunteer may go to the board to demonstrate another verb of the same type while you drill the forms orally, indicating the correct placement in the house. Varied pronouns should be drilled orally, such as él y yo, tú y yo, Juan y Marta, la maestra y él.

5. Now proceed to another group of verbs (B), explaining briefly why the change occurs. Follow the same steps.

6. Once students seem to comprehend the change, proceed to the third group of verbs (C), and present in the same manner as before.

7. Once all verbs have been covered, it is time for row drills. Ask the first student in each row to draw a house. Assign a verb from one of the three categories to each row.

8. The first student may place either the yo form or any form with which he or she is comfortable. All the following students place one form of their verb in their house.

9. Correction time begins. You can get students' attention and evaluative judgment by asking them to assign a number of correct answers per house.

10. Evaluate whether most students understand the concept or whether they need further clarification. Remind students that the spelling changes occur in the "basement" of the house. The term "basement boys" comes from the fact that the changes occur in the él and ellos zone of the house.

11. Homework should include a mixture of the verbs so that all the students get written practice using the spelling changes.

12. The following day, before correcting the homework—as a warmup activity—place houses on the board to ascertain whether there has been a carryover of learning from the previous day. Proceed as with row drills.

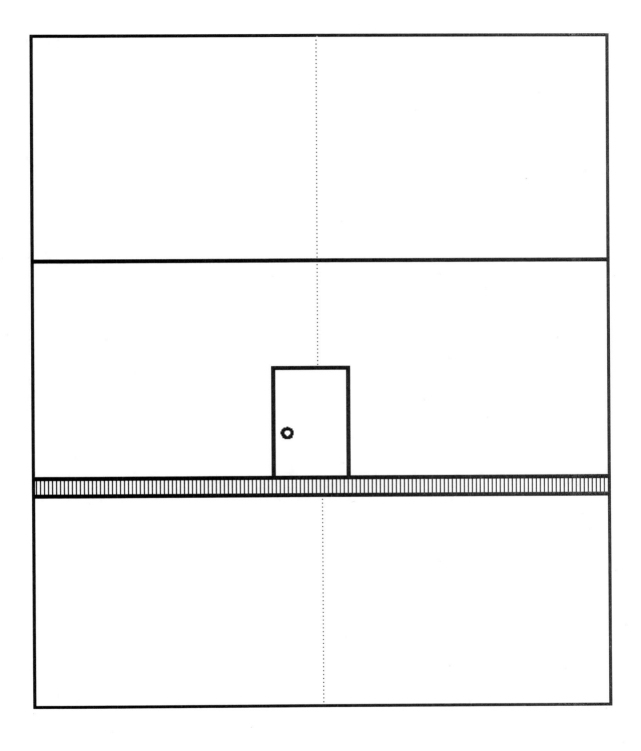

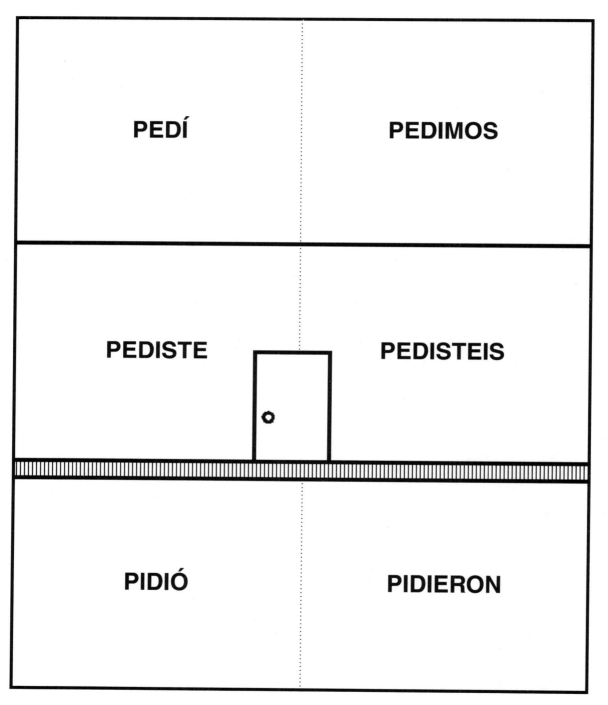

PEDÍ   PEDIMOS

PEDISTE   PEDISTEIS

PIDIÓ   PIDIERON

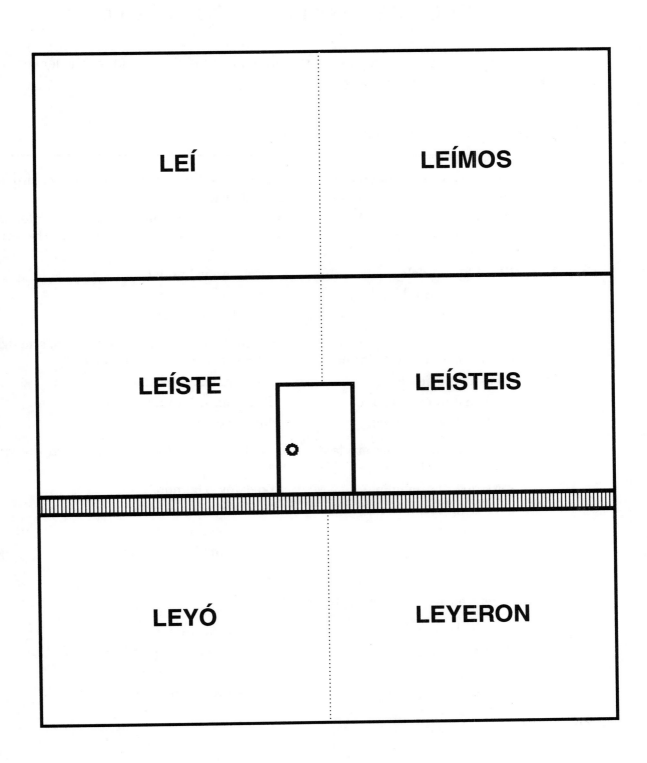

LEÍ

LEÍMOS

LEÍSTE

LEÍSTEIS

LEYÓ

LEYERON

EYEGLASSES: Present Progressive with Pronouns

For this activity, use eyeglasses; the pronouns fit on either side of the lenses, but not in the middle. (See also "Elbow Verbs.")

HOW TO USE THE VISUAL DIAGRAM

1. Draw some simple pairs of eyeglasses or use the transparency master provided—one on top of the other, or one beside the other.

2. On the first pair, put the pronoun(s) to the right of the present participle, and drill several examples. Point out that the pronouns are attached to the verb, thus requiring accents. Drill these exercises:

   Estoy haciéndolo.   Están escuchándolo.

   Están comprándomelo.   Estamos llamándote.

   No estoy comiéndolo.   No está mirándonos.

3. On the second pair, put the pronoun(s) to the left of the helping verb, and drill several examples. Point out that the pronouns are not attached.

   Lo estoy haciendo.   Lo están escuchando.

   Me lo están comprando.   Te estamos llamando.

   No lo estoy comiendo.   No nos está mirando.

4. Mix and match. Ask students to repeat the verb given, then switch the pronoun to the other side of the glasses.

   Estamos escribiéndolo.   Lo estoy pagando.

   ¿Me lo estás hablando?   Le están contestando.

   ¿Estás comiéndolo?   Estoy llamándote.

   No lo estoy leyendo.   No estamos repitiéndoselo.

5. Try some translations from English.

   Accept either position for the pronouns.

   I am watching it.   Isn't he eating it?

   We are calling you.   They are speaking to him.

   She isn't doing it.   He is buying it for her.

   Who is singing it?   We are watching him.

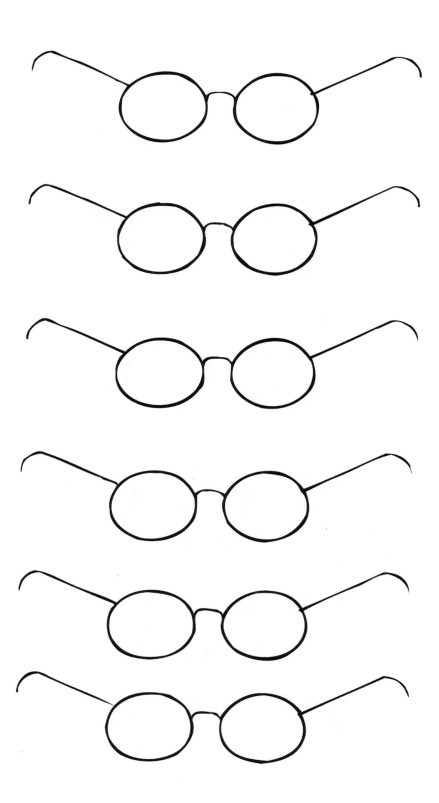

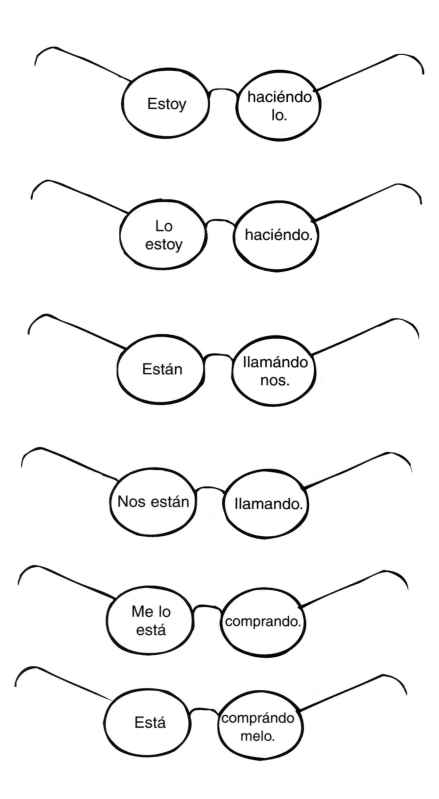

BOX: Imperfect vs. Preterit (Passé Composé)

As explained with the previous boxes, only the most basic and comprehensible rules will be presented. This is a particularly elusive and complex grammar topic; the other rules (for example, "general description")—which are vital to learn, and do need to be addressed—can be taught after mastery of the basic concept.

It is assumed here that formation of these two tenses has been taught and mastered before the differences are tackled.

HOW TO USE THE VISUAL DIAGRAM

1. Make four boxes, as shown in the reproducibles, and fill in the top left with USED TO. Give some English examples of what you used to do years ago.

2. Pointing to the box, repeat some examples in the foreign language with their time counterparts.

   Siempre comía dulces.   (Je les mangeais toujours.)

   Todos los días caminaba.   (Chaque jour je le faisais.)

   Cuando era joven lo jugaba.   (Quand j'étais jeune, j'y jouais.)

   Todos los domingos íbamos allí.   (Tous les dimanches nous y allions.)

3. Fill in the top right with DID, giving examples in English by asking questions about what the students did last night. For example, What did you eat last night? Did you do your homework?

4. Repeat some examples with their time counterparts.

   ¿Leíste el libro anoche?   (Tu as lu le livre hier soir?)

   ¿Miraste el programa ayer?   (Tu as vu l'émission hier?)

   ¿Lo leyeron anteayer?   (Je l'ai lu il y a deux jours.)

   ¿Ya comió el chico?   (Il a déjà mangé?)

5. Fill in the bottom left box with WAS (WERE)—ING and the bottom right box with -ED. Give some examples in English of the interruptive nature of the preterit (passé composé), most commonly expressed by -ED.

6. Repeat some sentences by moving the index finger from left to right or from right to left, as each sentence warrants.

   Los alumnos gritaban   cuando el director entró.

   Mientras comía   dejé caer el vaso.

   Mirábamos la televisión   cuando sonó el teléfono.

   (Il lisait son livre   quand le téléphone a sonné.)

   (Pendant que je mangeais   j'ai laissé tomber le verre.)

   (Je bavardais avec les clients   quand le patron est arrivé.)

7. Erase the four rules. Ask students to repeat them back. Write them as they say them, always keeping the rules in their original box.

8. Try some short sentences from English.

He used to walk.	I talked.	While you were sleeping. . . .
We arrived.	Did you eat?	I always used to watch it.

Note: At this point more exercises are needed for adequate drilling due to the difficulty of the concept.

IMPERFECTO	PRETÉRITO
USED TO	DID
WAS/WERE ...ING	-ED

IMPARFAIT	PASSÉ COMPOSÉ
USED TO	DID
WAS/WERE ...ING	-ED

WILL AND WOULD FISH: Future and Conditional

HOW TO USE THE VISUAL DIAGRAM

Start with the future fish visual diagram.

1. Give some examples of what the future tense sounds like in English. Tell the students that the future will now be called the "Will Fish."

2. On the empty fish visual diagram, fill in the bodies with an infinitive of regular verbs only, reserving the endings for the tail. Point out that the future involves the whole word plus ending, fish body, and tail. (The teacher of French will have to point out the omission of the e for re verbs. Drill with the exercises below.

   FRENCH   SPANISH

   je mangerai   nous parlerons   yo comeré   nosotros viviremos

   tu finiras   vous choisirez   tú vivirás

   il sortira   elles vendront   él nadará   ellas hablarán

3. Point to any one of the fish and ask the students for the meaning of the fish.

4. Orally drill each fish, pointing specifically at the ending.

5. Erase the endings. Have the class orally fill in the whole fish as you point to them on the visual.

6. Once students can recall the endings of the regular verbs, it is time for the exceptions in the pie at the bottom. This is the "Will Pie." Write the irregulars in the various sections of the pie.

7. After erasing the regular verbs in the fish visual diagram, place the root (from the pie) in each fish body. Drill each fish, complete with irregular root and already learned tail (ending).

   FRENCH   SPANISH

   je serai   nous saurons   yo diré   nosotros saldremos

   tu auras   vous pourrez   tú harás

   elle fera   ils iront   ella cabrá   ellos valdrán

8. Erase the irregular fish. Now ask students to hone in on the important irregulars by isolating one verb at a time, onto which they should practice all the future endings. Since there are only six fish on the visual yet at least nine irregular roots to drill, all the verbs must be drilled. These are commonly used verbs, and much oral practice is needed.

   FRENCH   SPANISH

   je verrai   nous verrons   yo tendré   nosotros tendremos

   tu verras   vous verrez   tú tendrás

   il verra   elles verront   él tendrá   ellas tendrán

Now substitute the other irregular verbs.

9. Try some translations from English, using regular and irregular fish.

He will watch.	They will eat.	He will not drink.
We will leave.	You will see.	I will cook.
What will you do?	When will he leave?	Who will be there?
We will have.	You will do.	She will know.

10. Repeat the translations but add a pronoun, perhaps "it."

| He will watch it. | They will eat it. | He will not drink it. |

11. Recap by saying "whole body plus tail" and "exceptions in the pie."

12. Now repeat the process by changing the future to conditional; call the new tense (or mode) the "Would Fish." Point out that the future and conditional fish are so similar that they are like cousins.

FRENCH   SPANISH

(Step 2)

| je mangerais | nous mangerions | yo comería | nosotros viviríamos |

(Step 7)

| je serais | nous saurions | yo diría | nosotros saldríamos |

(Step 8)

| je verrais | nous verrions | yo tendría | nosotros tendríamos |

(Step 9)

| He would watch. | They would eat. | He would not drink. |

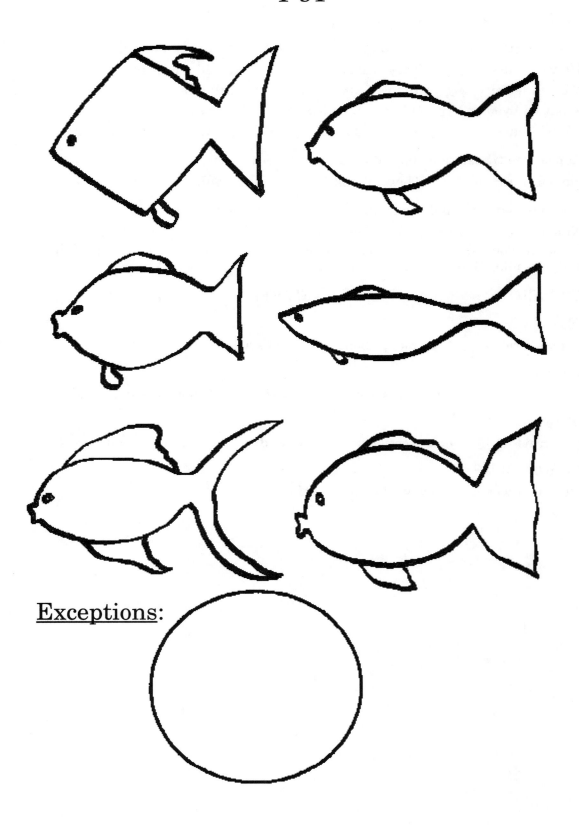

Exceptions:

1-52

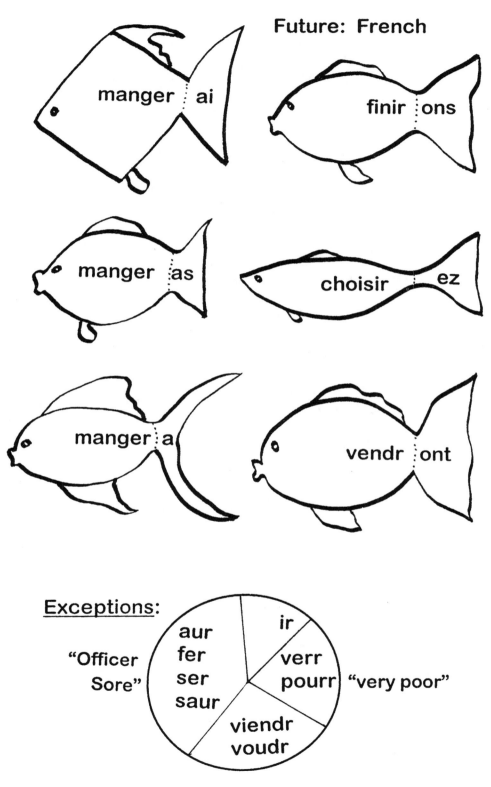

Future: French

manger | ai

finir | ons

manger | as

choisir | ez

manger | a

vendr | ont

Exceptions:

"Officer Sore"

aur
fer
ser
saur

ir

verr
pourr

"very poor"

viendr
voudr

©1996 by The Center for Applied Research in Education

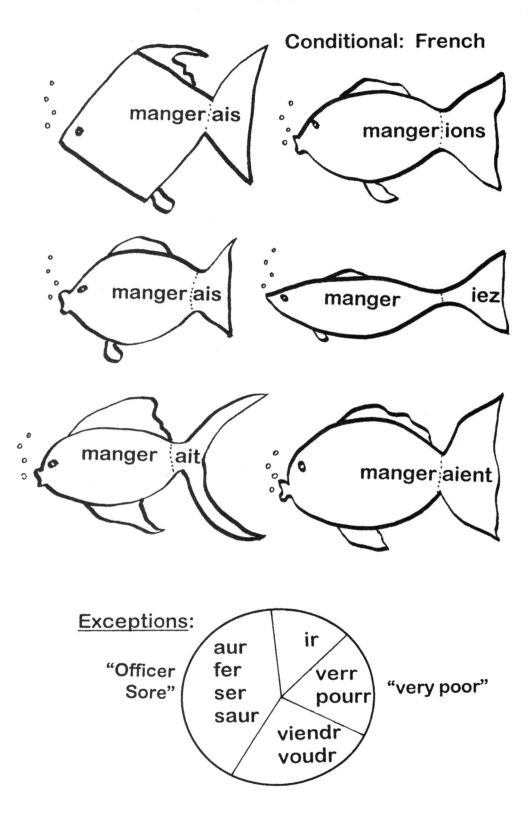

Conditional: French

manger ais

manger ions

manger ais

manger iez

manger ait

manger aient

©1996 by The Center for Applied Research in Education

Exceptions:

"Officer
Sore"

aur
fer
ser
saur

ir

verr
pourr

viendr
voudr

"very poor"

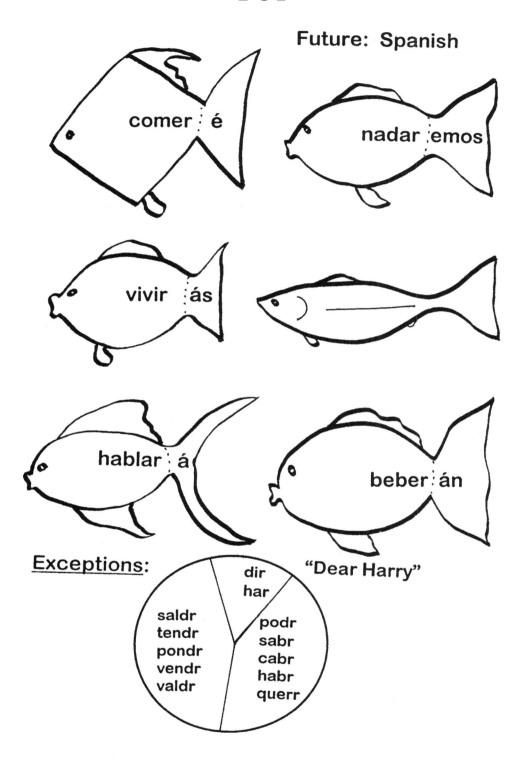

Future: Spanish

comer : é

nadar : emos

vivir : ás

hablar : á

beber : án

"Dear Harry"

Exceptions:

dir
har

saldr
tendr
pondr
vendr
valdr

podr
sabr
cabr
habr
querr

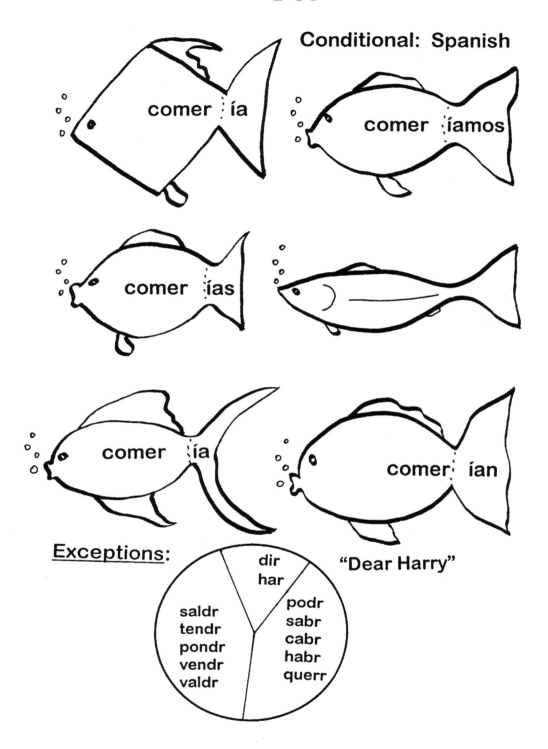

Conditional: Spanish

comer · ía

comer · íamos

comer · ías

comer · ía

comer · ían

Exceptions: "Dear Harry"

dir
har

podr
sabr
cabr
habr
querr

saldr
tendr
pondr
vendr
valdr

GRID: Future and Conditional

PURPOSE: Drill for future and conditional irregular stems

HOW TO USE THE VISUAL DIAGRAM

1. Distribute a xeroxed empty grid to students.
2. Ask students to provide the root for the following verbs if they have already learned this. If this is an initial presentation of the irregular stems, provide the verbal and written stems.

   DECIR   HACER (These have three letters in their root.)

   SABER   CABER   HABER   PODER (These have four letters.)

   SALIR   VALER   PONER   VENIR   TENER   QUERER

   (These six verbs have five letters in their root.)
3. Place the root in the grid by using one letter per box, as in the diagram.
4. After the three-lettered roots are written in, write in the four- and five-lettered roots. Students should do this while you write them on the overhead.
5. There are other verbs that may be added to this list. These, however, are the usual verbs presented in the texts.
6. Further verbal activities may now be needed to practice these roots with their endings.

1-56

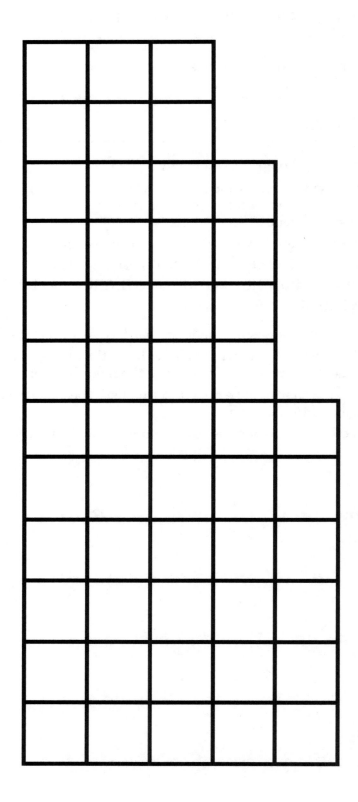

D	I	R		
H	A	R		
C	A	B	R	
H	A	B	R	
P	O	D	R	
S	A	B	R	
P	O	N	D	R
Q	U	E	R	R
S	A	L	D	R
T	E	N	D	R
V	A	L	D	R
V	E	N	D	R

CLOCK: Irregular Future and Conditional Forms

PURPOSE: To drill the meaning of irregular future and conditional endings

HOW TO USE THE VISUAL DIAGRAM

1. Drawing the clock on the board or using the overhead transparency, put the translation of I WILL or I WOULD in the center.

2. Place the translations of the other irregular verbs around the clock. That is, place the native language translations, as per the diagram. If all the irregulars have not been taught, include some regulars so that there is one verb per hour on the clock.

3. With a pointer, start at 12:00. Have the students chorally call out as you proceed from 12:00 to 1:00 to 2:00, and so forth, until the whole clock has been covered.

4. You may wish to call upon individuals or students in rows to give the desired target language word.

5. Change the center to read whatever the desired subject is: HE WILL, THEY WOULD, WE WILL.

6. The oral drill is an essential part of mastering the concept. This overhead or drill can be used as a warmup activity, especially after a long vacation, when students tend to feel that they remember nothing.

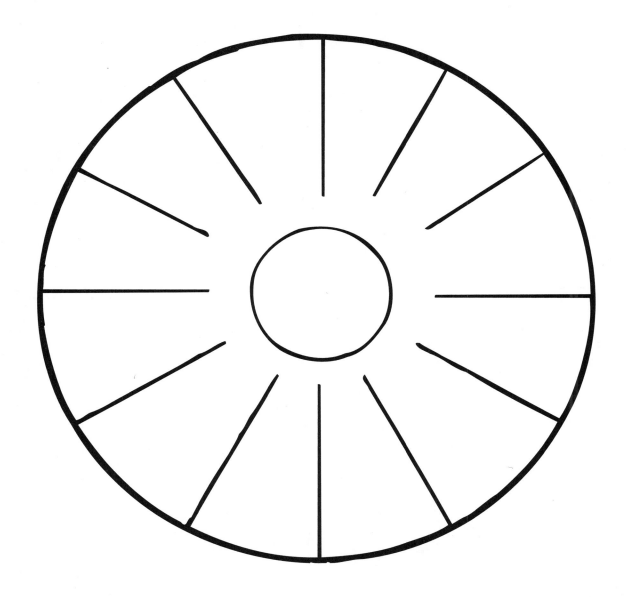

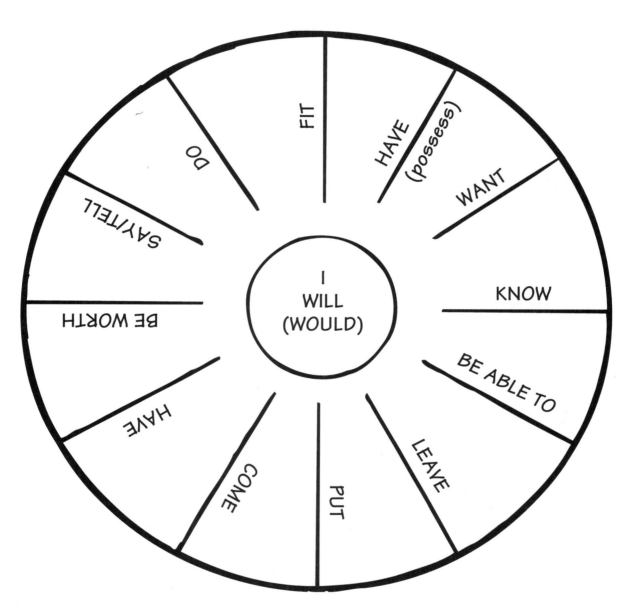

BRIDGE AND STATES: The Subjunctive

This abstract and complicated topic, so unfamiliar in usage to our students, needs much exposure to the concept and extensive drill. To open their minds, the bridge and two states will be used to drill the initial patterns. You will have to precede this lesson, however, with lessons on the formation of the subjunctive (taken perhaps from the "Command Snake" in this book), as well as follow it with multiple drills on the reasons for the subjunctive. This lesson is, once again, only a mind opener.

HOW TO USE THE VISUAL DIAGRAM

1. Establish the idea that <u>one state</u> represents one subject doing both verbs, which means, "Don't conjugate the second verb!" "Use the infinitive of the second verb." <u>Two states</u> refers to two different subjects, each with their own conjugated verb. Inform students that the state on the right has two main roads. Once the bridge, represented by QUE is crossed, students must choose between the old indicative road (southbound) or the new subjunctive road (northbound). And how will students know which road to take? They must take their cue from a message in the state to the left. The pattern is based on the map of New Jersey, the George Washington Bridge, and New York.

2. Across the top on the visual diagrams, write and drill orally some <u>one state</u> sentences with infinitives such as:

FRENCH	SPANISH
Je sais <u>écrire</u>.	Yo sé <u>patinar</u>.
Tu veux <u>sortir</u>?	¿Tú quieres <u>salir</u>?
Il ne veut pas <u>manger</u>.	El no desea <u>comer</u>.

You may choose to write these with colored markers. Green could represent infinitives and red could represent conjugated verbs, as in "<u>Stop</u> and think which road to take!"

3. Across the middle, write and drill orally some sentences with mixed subjunctive and indicative. Subjunctive verbs, emanating from North Jersey, go north. Indicative verbs, emananting from South Jersey, go south.

FRENCH	SPANISH
Je sais qu'ils vont.	Yo sé que ellos van.
Je doute qu'ils aillent.	Yo dudo que ellos vayan.
Il croit que nous le faisons.	El cree que lo hacemos.
Il ne croit pas que nous le fassions.	El no cree que lo hagamos.

4. After drilling these sentences, elicit from the students <u>why</u> there are conjugated vs. infinitive structures. The answer should be "the use of the same subject for both verbs, thus no QUE, no need to cross the bridge into another state," and "the use of different subjects for the two verbs, thus the need for QUE." If the students don't perceive the difference, point out that QUE indicates the use of two different subjects—one on the left side of the verb, another on the right.

5. If students need some reinforcement on this concept, try a few English sentences to see if they can discriminate between one- and two-subject sentences; for example, given the following sentences, is each one a "stay in New Jersey—infinitive" or a "go to New York—conjugated verb"?

EXAMPLES:

I want to leave.	He wants me to leave.
He knows how to swim.	She doubts that I swim.
We need to eat.	We ask them to eat.

The bridge concept should now be taught; that is, once the students see the word QUE, the bridge, they must decide whether to take the subjunctive road or the indicative road. It is up to you to determine how many, and which rules will be taught initially. Begin with certain rules that require the "new road" (the subjunctive), then contrast them with the "old road" (the indicative). My own classes have been exposed to "heart and doubt" words for the "new road." They see a heart for emotions and volition, and a question mark for doubt words, as in the exercises.

NEW ROAD (Place a (♥) and a (?) above the verbs on the left of each sentence on the visual.) Remind students that North Jersey heart and doubt words take the north route in New York.

FRENCH	SPANISH
Je doute qu'il le fasse.	Yo dudo que él lo haga.
Il ne croit pas que je finisse.	El no cree que yo termine.
Nous voulons qu'il le fasse.	Queremos que él lo haga.
Je ne veux pas qu'il le fasse.	Yo no quiero que él lo haga.
Papa veut que je finisse.	Papá quiere que yo termine.

(This list should be expanded at a later time.)

OLD ROAD: Point out that the trigger words devoid of emotions and doubt emanate from South Jersey and take the southern route in New York. Write these sentences across the bottom of the visual.

FRENCH	SPANISH
Je crois qu'ils le feront.	Creo que ellos lo harán.
Il sait que je le fais.	Papá sabe que yo lo hago.
Nous pensons qu'il est jeune.	Pensamos que él es joven.

6. Try some contrasting sentences: indicative vs. subjunctive.

Student will reply with: <u>yo haga</u> or <u>yo hago</u> (Spanish) or <u>je fais</u> or <u>je fasse</u> (French).

FRENCH	SPANISH
Il veut que. . . .	El quiere que. . . .
Il croit que. . . .	El cree que. . . .
Maman doute que. . . .	Mamá duda que. . . .
Maman ne veut pas que. . . .	Mamá no quiere que. . . .
Ils savent que. . . .	Ellos necesitan que. . . .
Il souhaite que. . . .	Tienen miedo de que. . . .

7. Try some English translation drills.

He wants to go.	He wants me to go.
I want to go.	I want him to go.
They need to study.	They ask me to study.
We want to leave.	We want her to leave.
I know how to swim.	I know that she swims.
Can you write?	He is sure that I know.

8. Recapitulate using the visuals:

Staying in the left state requires only one conjugated verb.

Moving from left to right state indicates two separate subjects, thus two separate conjugated verbs.

Once the QUE bridge is crossed, a subjunctive or indicative route through the new state is required. Refer to the state on the left for that decision.

1-60

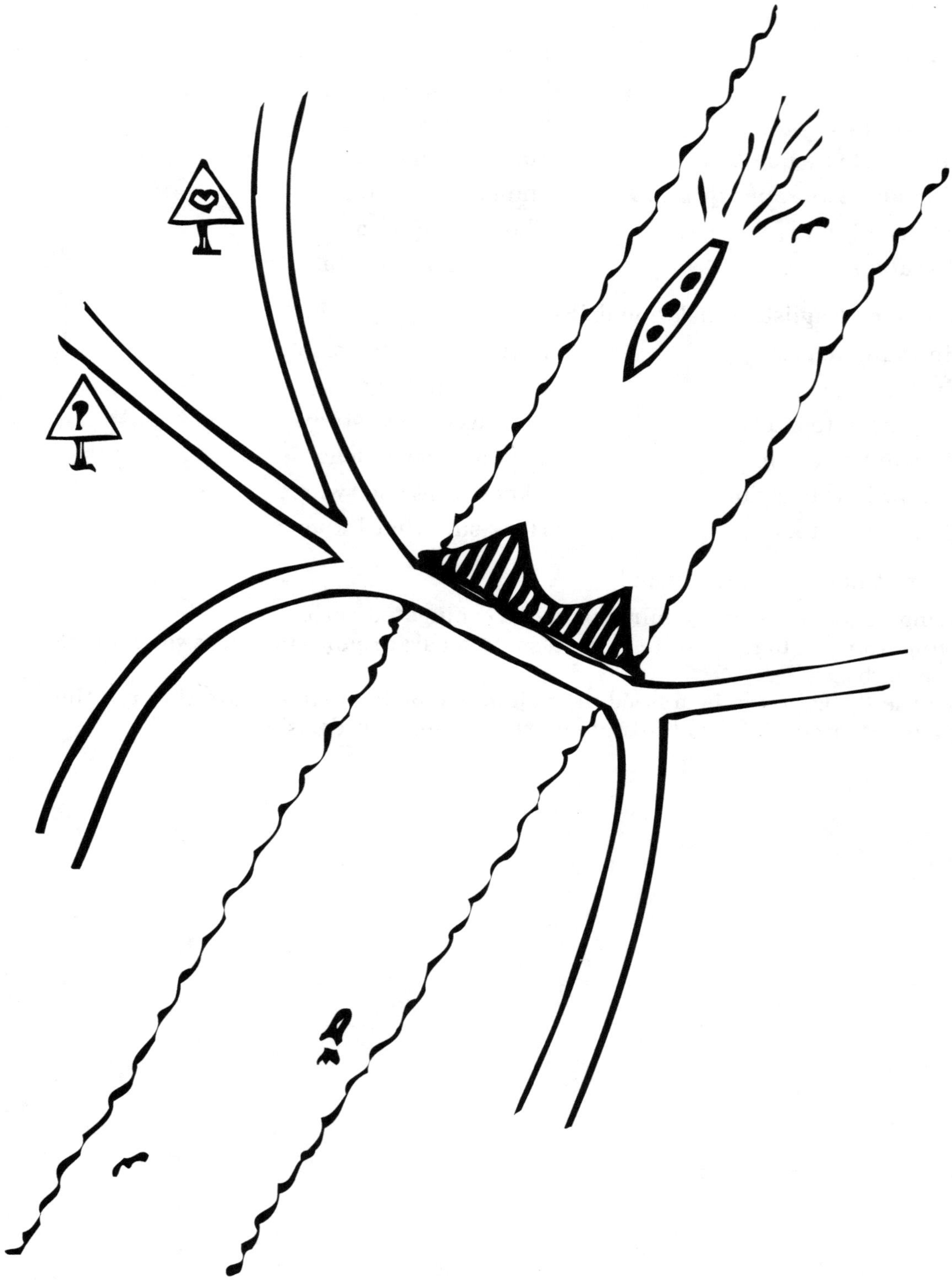

1-61

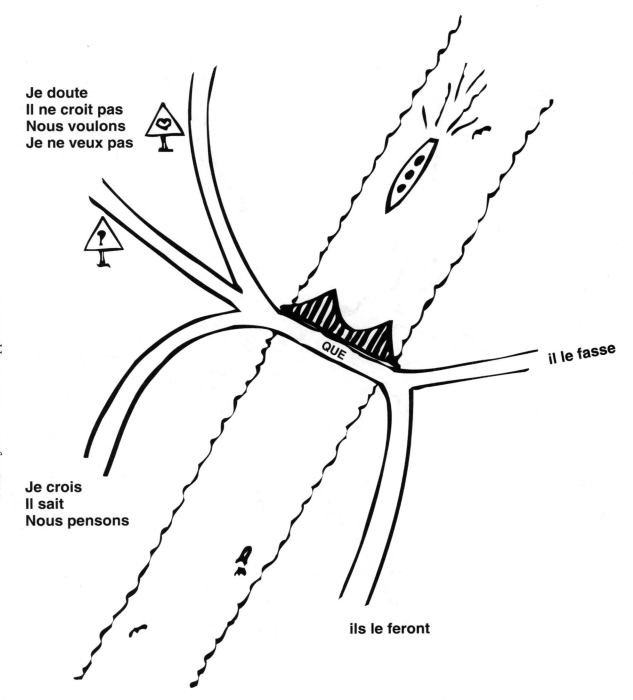

Je doute
Il ne croit pas
Nous voulons
Je ne veux pas

Je crois
Il sait
Nous pensons

QUE

il le fasse

ils le feront

1-62

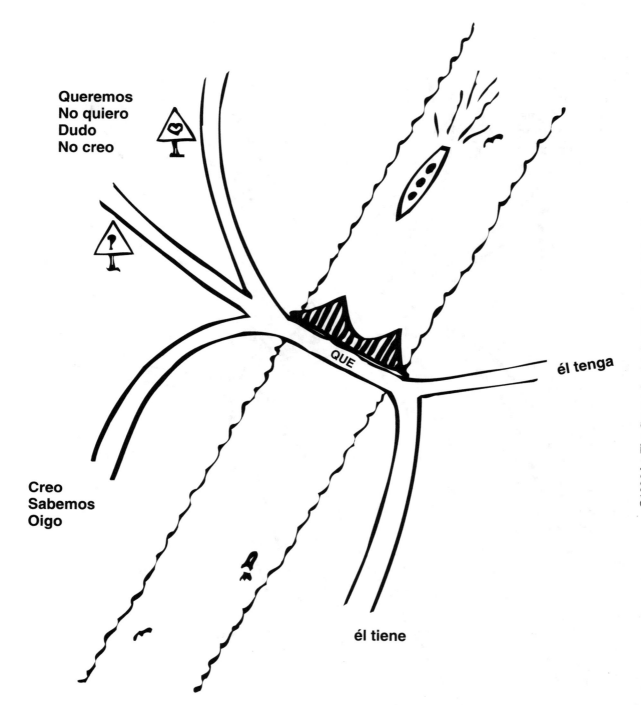

Queremos
No quiero
Dudo
No creo

Creo
Sabemos
Oigo

QUE

él tenga

él tiene

ORBITS: Subjunctive vs. Indicative

INTRODUCTION: The "Bridge and States" image should establish the critical aspects of the subjunctive. "Orbits" should follow up—a simple drill so that automatic language habits can be developed to stress the difference between the subjunctive and the indicative.

HOW TO USE THE VISUAL DIAGRAM

1. Insert a subjunctive setup or "trigger word" on each satellite at the outer circle.

   For Spanish:

1. Yo quiero	2. El prefiere	3. Ellos lamentan
4. Nos enojamos de	5. Ella se alegra de	

   For French:

1. J'aime	2. Il préfère	3. Nous regrettons
4. Ils détestent	5. Elle ne croit pas	

2. On the next circle shown on the visual diagram, put the infinitive form of several common verbs, opposite each one of the planets or satellites. Infinitives could include pronouns, if desired.

   For Spanish:

1. salir	2. escribirle	3. hacerlo
4. sentarnos	5. venir	

   For French:

1. être	2. le faire	3. avoir
4. aller	5. pouvoir	

3. Start at the 12:00 position (for Spanish) and orally drill by repeating:

   For Spanish:

1. Yo quiero salir.	2. El prefiere escribirle.
3. Ellos lamentan hacerlo.	4. Nos enojamos de sentarnos.
5. Ella se alegra de venir.	

   For French:

1. J'aime être. . . .	2. Il préfère le faire. . . .
3. Nous regrettons avoir. . . .	4. Ils détestent aller. . . .
5. Elle ne croit pas pouvoir. . . .	

4. On the inner circle, at points opposite the infinitive, use a change of subject, preferably the "you" form, and the subjunctive form of the verb in the first orbit. Write the form, then practice orally.

For Spanish:	R E P E A T:
1. que (tú) salgas	Quiero que (tú) salgas.
2. que (tú) le escribas	El prefiere que (tú) le escribas.
3. que (tú) lo hagas	Ellos lamentan que (tú) lo hagas.
4. que (tú) te sientes	Nos enojamos de que (tú) te sientes.
5. que (tú) vengas	Ella se alegra de que (tú) vengas.

For French:	R E P E A T:
1. que tu sois	J'aime que tu sois. . . .
2. que tu le fasses	Il préfère que tu le fasses.
3. que tu aies	Nous regrettons que tu aies. . . .
4. que tu ailles	Ils détestent que tu ailles.
5. que tu puisses	Elle ne croit pas que tu puisses. . . .

5. Work backwards, or clockwise, and repeat the complete sentences.

6. Using a mix-and-match format where possible, give students some English clues to elicit the Spanish or French.

To ascertain a comprehension between infinitive and subjunctive structure:

For Spanish:

1. I want you	to do it.
2. He prefers	to do it.
3. We regret	leaving.
4. We're angry	that you're leaving.
5. I want	to leave.

For French:

1. We're sorry	that you do it.
2. She doesn't believe	that you go.
3. They hate	being. . . .
4. He prefers	to be. . . .
5. I love	doing it.

7. If the "Orbits" drill is extremely effective, you may consider creating orbits that require the <u>indicative</u>, to serve as a point of contrast to the situations requiring the subjunctive.

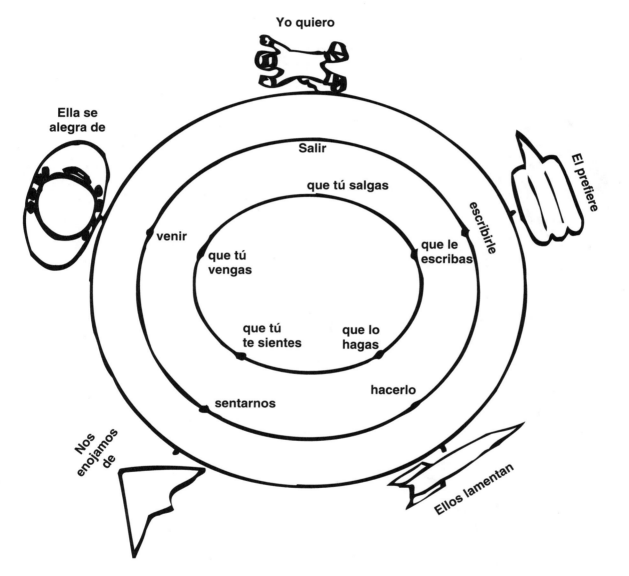

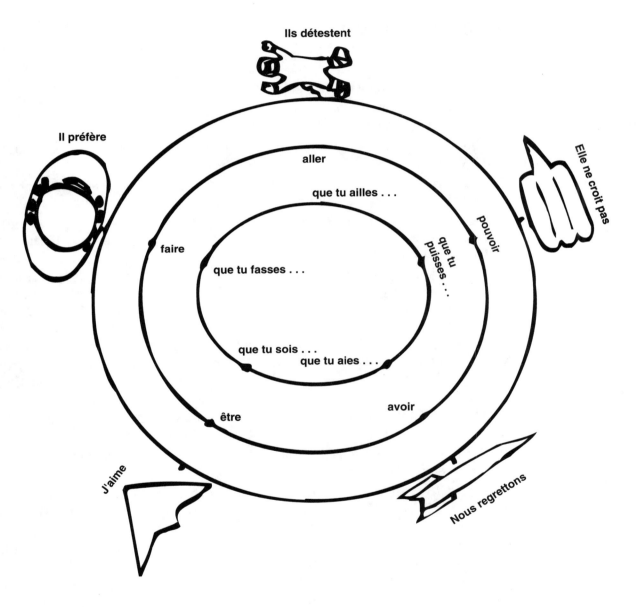

PLANT: A Short Verb Tense Synopsis—Spanish

INTRODUCTION: Students mix up verb forms. A tenga or tendré appears where tengo is needed. To help clarify verb meaning or tense derivation, or for a quick review, take a common regular or irregular verb. Present some basic tenses using the yo form and a plant with offshoots.

HOW TO USE THE VISUAL DIAGRAM

1. Using the visual diagram of a plant, entitle it with the name of the verb to be highlighted. For this exercise, start with DECIR.

2. At the root area of the plant, request the yo form of the present, or ask how one says "I say." Write the answer at the root.

3. On the left offshoot, request the yo form of the preterit, or ask how one says "I said." Write the answer on the space to the left.

4. On the right offshoot, request the yo form of the imperfect, or ask how one says "I used to say," or "I was saying." Write on the space to the right.

5. At the second level to the left ask students for the tú affirmative command, or how to say "say!" Remind students to cut away many letters of the verb DECIR. Write in the space.

6. On the stalk, between the left and right offshoots, request the usted command, or how to say "say!" Write in the space. Remind or show students that the usted command is derived from the yo present tense and that the ending vowel is "flipped." Er verbs use an a. Ar verbs use an E.

7. To the right, request the subjunctive of TU, EL, NOSOTROS, ELLOS. The "YO" form has been provided by the answer to Step #6. Write in the space to the right. Point out the similarities between the USTED command and the subjunctive.

8. At level three to the right, request the conditional form, or how to say "I WOULD SAY." Write the answer as in the visual. Point out the similarity in endings between the conditional and the imperfect.

9. Still at level three to the right, above the conditional, request the future form, or how to say "I WILL SAY," then write it.

10. Finally, in the last space to the right, request the present perfect form, or how to say " I HAVE SAID." Point out that the future endings will have the same endings as HABER forms, minus the "H", but adding accents.

11. After this plant has been completed, try another verb, regular or irregular. Always keep the tenses in the same position.

12. This particular drill can be used as a warmup or as a row drill. If used as a row drill, each row would have a plant to fill out at the board. The first person in each row would be responsible for the present tense, the second person, the preterit, and so forth. Variations can be made for other subject pronouns.

13. Remember to keep the same plant design to serve as "training wheels" for those students who are confused by so many different verb tenses.

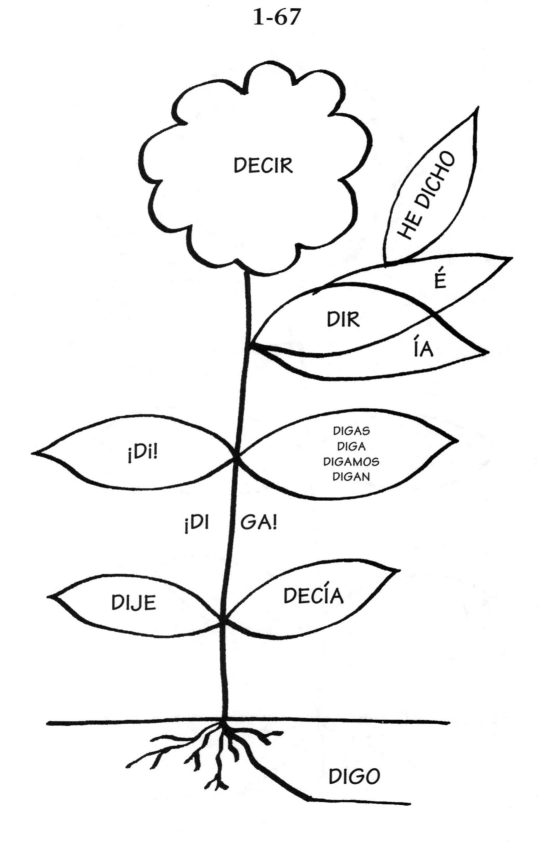

¡Hágaselo!

Se lo hice.

¡No se lo haga!

Voy a hacérselo.

COMBINATION TENSES & PRONOUNS

Faites-le-lui!

Ne le lui faites pas!

Je le lui ai fait.

Je vais le lui faire.

LIGHTNING BOLT: Past Tense and Pronoun Drill

HOW TO USE THE VISUAL DIAGRAM

1. On the board draw a simple lightning bolt, or use an overhead transparency for each row in class. Follow the model by placing a present tense verb with a pronoun on each level. This is interesting to do in French because of all the agreement with various preceding direct object pronouns or with subjects.

2. Students should write the past tense on the line underneath the present tense. They can write the next one in line, or one that they feel comfortable writing.

3. When you focus the class on correcting the responses, the level that caused an error can be erased. You or the class should provide the correct answer. Because each level tests at least two items, both items should be completely correct.

4. Keep a note of where the errors are made—of which concepts have still not been mastered. When you repeat the drill the same day or on a subsequent day, the levels that caused errors should have the same type of sentence in the same space. For example, if on level 4 the student did not place the proper agreement onto the verb, that level (4) should then contain another difficulty of the same type. In French, it may be a reflexive verb.

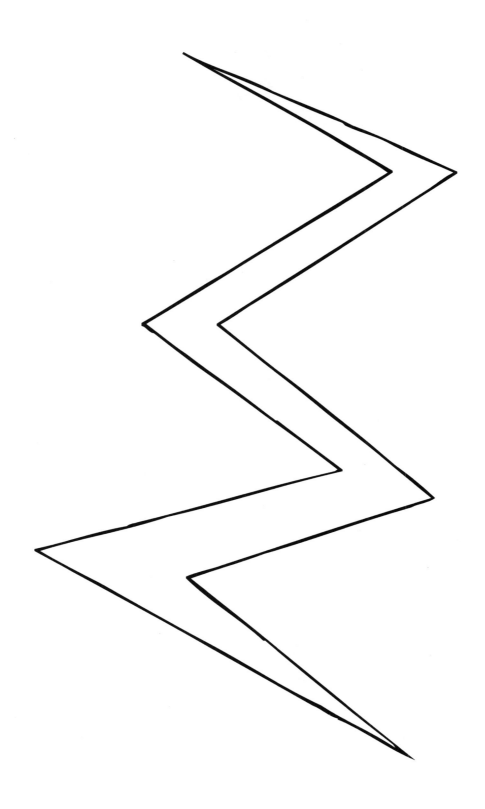

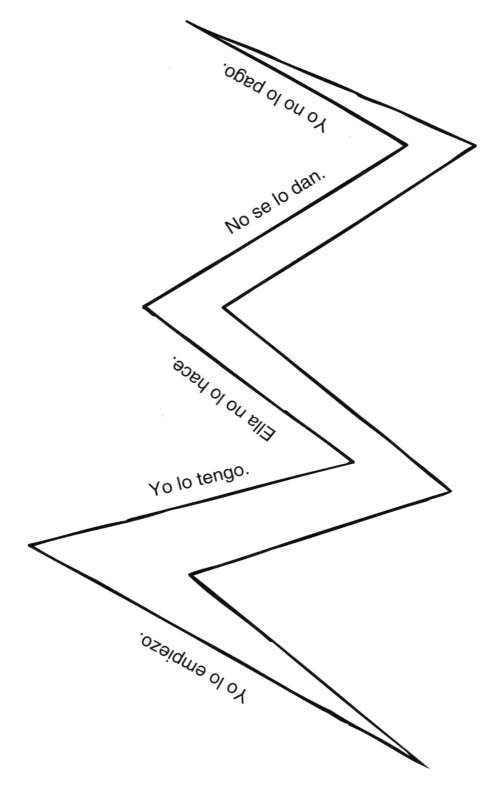

Yo no lo pago.

No se lo dan.

Ella no lo hace.

Yo lo tengo.

Yo lo empiezo.

WINDOW PANES: Verb Tense with Pronoun Placement

HOW TO USE THE VISUAL DIAGRAM

1. Provide each student with a copy of the reproducible of four boxes representing window panes.

2. Ask for

   a. a present tense and pronoun for the top left pane,

   b. the past tense of the first verbal idea in the top right,

   c. the affirmative command (formal) and pronoun for the bottom left pane,

   d. and the negative command with the pronoun in the bottom right pane.

   (Start with commonly known verbs.)

a. I watch it.	b. I watched it.
c. Watch it!	d. Don't watch it!

   (Try an irregular verb.)

a. He does it!	b. He did it!
c. Do it!	d. Don't do it!

   (Try a verb with a double object pronoun.)

a. I buy it for her.	b. I bought it for her.
c. Buy it for her!	d. Don't buy it for her!

   In an additional exercise, use a double verb combination along the lines of the window panes, forming a cross. For example, you could request the following verbal ideas:

I have to work.	I am going to work.
He is working.	He begins to work.

3. The students should exchange papers.

4. As you elicit from the class the correct answer for each window pane, the correctors should shatter the window pane by crossing it out if it contains an incorrect answer.

5. Walk around the room to inspect how many panes were shattered, and where they occurred, that is, which structure caused the greatest number of errors.

6. For goal orientation, repeat the exercise by expressing the desire to see improvement, but first, students should practice the four correct answers orally with you. Be sure to use some irregular verbs and some with double object pronouns.

7. Always keep the same verb tense in the same window pane. If students continue to make errors in the same window pane, they will be able to identify their nemesis, which is the first step in correcting the problem.

ELBOW VERBS: Verb and Infinitive and Pronouns—Spanish

Prior to teaching this concept define the concept of "elbow verbs" to the students. They are double verbs—one conjugated and the other an infinitive—often separated by another small word such as <u>a</u>, <u>que</u>, or <u>de</u>.

HOW TO USE THE VISUAL DIAGRAM

1. Draw some large elbows on the board, or use the transparency master. Place object pronouns first in the hand, drilling this pattern as follows:

Lo voy a hacer.	Lo tengo que hacer.
Me va a llamar.	Te voy a escribir.
Le van a hablar.	Lo acabo de terminar.
Lo quiero comer.	¿No lo quieres comer?

2. Then place the pronouns close to the shoulder—following, but attached to, the verb in the infinitive form. State that this position is also possible. Drill this form.

Voy a hacerlo.	Tengo que hacerlo.
Va a llamarme.	Voy a escribirte.
Van a hablarle.	Acabo de terminarlo.
Quiero comerlo.	¿No quieres comerlo?

3. Mix and match placements by giving the "pronoun in the hand" when you want the "pronoun by the shoulder," and vice versa. As if plotting the item, point to the hand or shoulder to help the students visualize the pattern.

Me van a llamar.	Vamos a hacerlo.
¿Nos vas a cantar?	Voy a cantarles.
Tengo que hacerlo.	Lo acaban de mirar.
Me enseñan a jugar.	Aprenden a hacerlo.

4. Remind students not to divorce the verbs, that is, no pronouns come between the verbs, *nothing* on the elbow joint. "Front or back. If you put it in the middle, then smack, smack, smack."

5. Try some double object pronouns.

   (Point out whether the shoulder or the hand has been chosen in each item given orally.)

Van a comprármelo.	Tienen que mandárnoslo.
Acaban de prestárselos.	¿Me lo vas a dar?
¿Te lo va a hacer?	¿Quieres dármelo?

6. Try some English translations.

I want to eat it.	He has to call me.
We want to buy it for her.	They just bought it.
Are you going to do it?	We are going to tell it to them.

7. This can now be used with the present progressive tense, but it must be drilled orally as it is visualized.

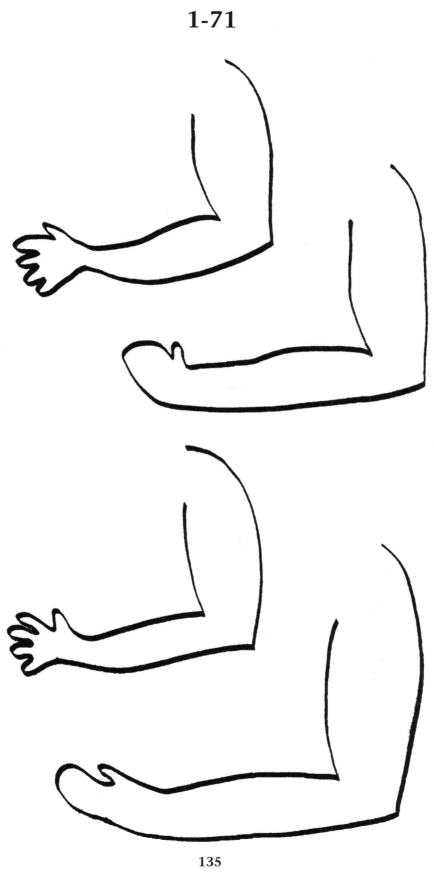

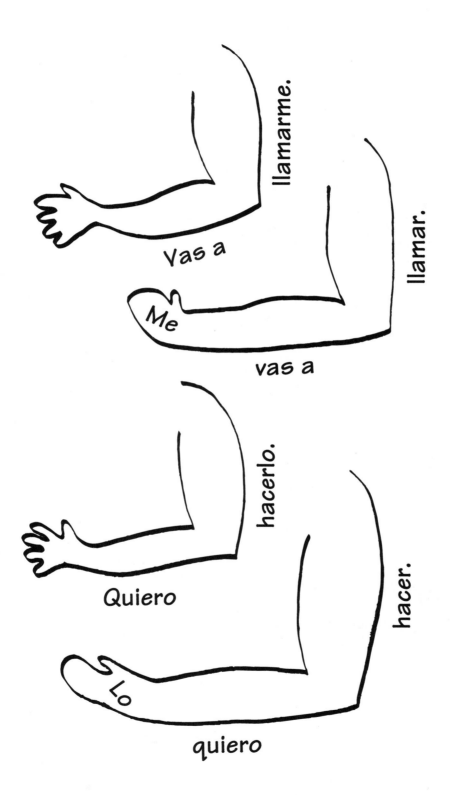

Vas a

llamarme.

llamar.

Me

vas a

hacerlo.

Quiero

hacer.

Lo

quiero

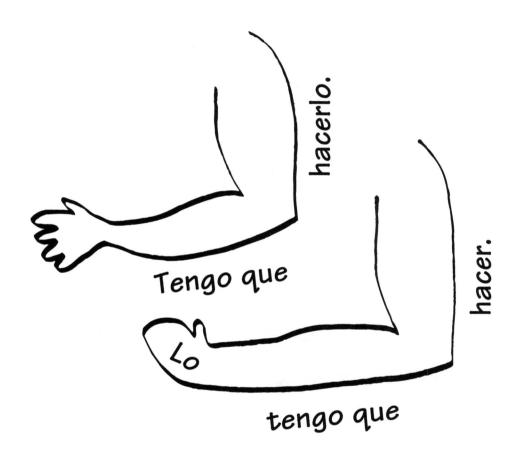

APPLES & ORCHARDS: Tense and Pronouns—French

Most grammar books explain with great detail the position of pronouns. Unless the placements are drilled to the point of fluency, this difficult concept is not well learned.

The visual diagram helps anchor the concept, along with the vital oral drills.

HOW TO USE THE VISUAL DIAGRAMS

1. Explain that the apples represent pronouns, and the trees represent verbs.

2. Ask several key questions. In the first tree above, describe the apple to the verb. With "in front" as the answer, elicit the name of the tenses (passé composé, negative command, present). Then practice these models, using the exercises.

Je le veux	Je l'ai vu.	Ne l'achetez pas!
Tu le manges?	Il l'a acheté.	Ne l'écoutez pas!
Ils le vendent.	Tu l'as bu?	Ne le finissez pas!
Ils ne le vendent pas.	Tu ne l'as pas bu?	
Je ne le veux pas.	Je ne l'ai pas vu.	

3. In the second tree in the middle, describe the apple to the verb. With "behind" as the answer, name this orchard as "affirmative commands," then drill this model.

Achetez-le!	Regarde-le!	Ecoutez-le!
Finissez-le!	Vendez-le!	Choisis-le!

4. In the last tree, describe the apple to the verb. Given the answer of "in the middle" of two verbs (or double verbs), practice this model.

Je veux l'écouter.	Tu ne sais pas le lire?
Ils vont le vendre.	Je ne veux pas le dire.
Nous n'allons pas le finir.	Ils ne veulent pas le manger.
Il ne veut pas l'écouter.	Nous ne savons pas le dire.

5. On the second visual, with apples, ask students to imagine the pronoun LE in each apple, then orally drill these sentences with them.

6. On the third visual, without the apples to indicate placement, ask students to orally place the pronoun LE in the correct spot. This could also be a review homework sheet.

7. If there are any errors, the teacher should say "wrong tree." Another student should try until all trees are correct.

8. Recap by saying "Front, back, and in between."

9. Try some English translations. Students do get bogged down by the formation of the tenses.

I want to do it.	Do it!
I did it.	I can't do it.
Don't watch it!	Don't take it!
He sings it.	They don't sell it.

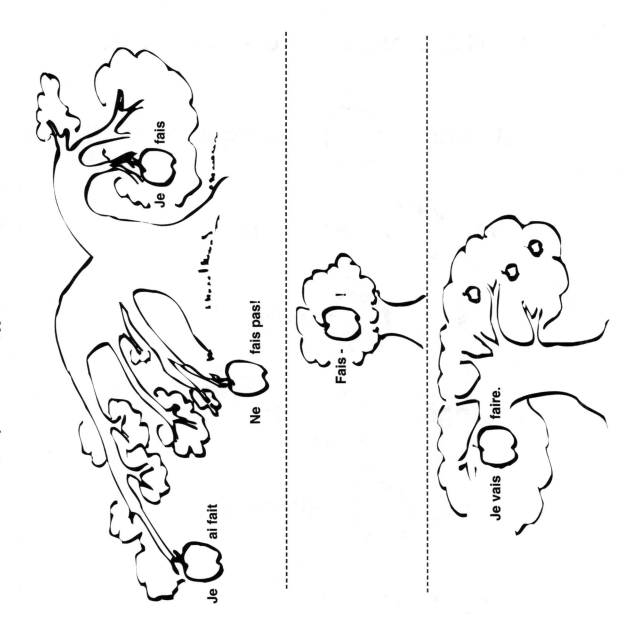

Insert a pronoun into each apple:

1. Ils vont manger.

2. Ne prenez pas!

3. Je sais faire.

4. Mangez- !

5. Nous avons vu.

6. Regardons- !

INSERT A PRONOUN INTO EACH SENTENCE

1.   **Regardons**   **!**

2. **Ne**   **prenez**   **pas!**

3. **Ils**   **vont**   **manger.**

4. **Nous**   **avons**   **vu.**

5. **Je ne**   **vais pas**   **faire.**

6.   **Mangez**   **!**

"LOUIS": FALLOIR structure—French

HOW TO USE THE VISUAL DIAGRAM

1. Give some English definitions to establish meaning, as in, Do you need? Do they need? What did she need? They will need.

2. Point out the name, LOUIS, and mention that the name is a reminder to use the lui system of indirect object pronouns.

3. Write the indirect object pronouns in the face.

4. Drill all pronouns with the present tense of il faut. Point out that "he" and "she" will both take lui, and that both forms of "they" will take leur.

   EXAMPLES:

   Il me faut. Il te faut. Il lui faut de l'argent. Il nous faut étudier. Il leur faut.

5. On the lines, fill out the verb tenses already learned by the students and drill ME with these tenses. (The IL VA FALLOIR can be taught at the end of these drills since the pronoun comes between the verbs.)

   EXAMPLES:

   Il m'a fallu étudier. Il me faudrait sortir. Il me faudra travailler. Il me fallait manger souvent.

6. Drill all the pronouns and tenses in a mix-and-match format.

   EXAMPLES:

   Il t'a fallu finir. Il leur faudra travailler. Il nous faudrait étudier. Il vous fallait corriger la phrase.

7. Drill all the pronouns and tenses from English, if desired.

FALLOIR: To need/To be necessary

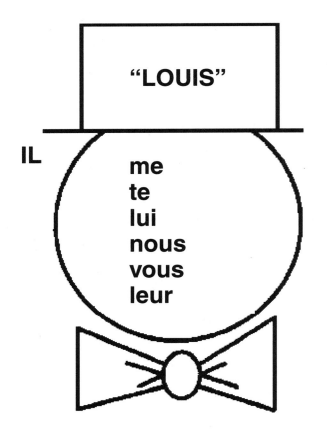

"LOUIS"

IL

me	faut.
te	fallait.
lui	a fallu.
nous	faudra.
vous	faudrait.
leur	avait fallu.

FALLOIR: To need/To be necessary

comparatives

superlatives

por vs. para

gustar

prepositional phrases

prepositions

MISCELLANEOUS

syntax

plurals

savoir vs. connaître

VERTICALS: Syntax

PURPOSE: To aid in the establishment of word placement in a sentence; to help focus on interrogative syntax, and for variety

PROCEDURE

1. On the board or overhead transparency, write four horizontal lines on which four sentence parts will be written, in list form, so that the sentences will be written in a vertical format, rather than a horizontal one.

2. Ask students to fill in each line with a predetermined word or idea given by you. For example, you can ask the students to write in the target language the following:

on line 1	WHY
on line 2	DO YOU COME
on line 3	LATE
on line 4	TO SCHOOL?

3. Correct the sentences before going on to the second attempt. Ask student volunteers to repeat what they wrote on each line. Write the answers, with the correct punctuation, at the board or on the overhead.

4. Ascertain how many have a perfect paper, perhaps by walking around the classroom.

5. In mixed-ability classes, there will be errors, and a second attempt will be necessary. Ask students to write the following:

on line 1	WHERE
on line 2	DO YOU GO
on line 3	EVERY DAY
on line 4	AFTER SCHOOL?

6. Correct as in the example above. Then check whether there has been an improvement.

7. If a third example is needed, try one with a negative such as:

on line 1	WHY
on line 2	DON'T YOU COME
on line 3	EARLY
on line 4	TO THE PARTY?

8. When students indicate improvement, ask them to build a four-piece sentence on the models they have already written.

9. Ask students to read their sentences aloud.

10. Finally, ask students to rewrite each of the sentences above in the normal horizontal format.

1-80

VERTICALS:

SENTENCE 1:   **SENTENCE 2:**   **SENTENCE 3:**

_____   _____   _____

_____   _____   _____

_____   _____   _____

_____   _____   _____

HORIZONTAL REWRITES:

1. _____

2. _____

3. _____

DELI SANDWICHES: Double Verb Combinations

PURPOSE: To help drill the double verb combinations that take "something in the middle," or nothing at all

INTRODUCTION: This grammar topic, usually presented in a list format, requires pure memorization. To spice up the presentation you might choose this more visual manner of accomplishing the same purpose as that of a list.

HOW TO USE THE VISUAL DIAGRAM

1. Draw four (or more, depending upon the number of combinations desired) sandwiches on the board or make a transparency from the reproducible. Three have space for filling, and one does not. This latter one will be the diet sandwich, with nothing in the middle.

2. Tell students that the second verb, an infinitive, is generally preceded by a preliminary word, or use easier words to say the same thing.

3. Place a filling such as QUE between the slices of one sandwich with TENER on the top piece of bread. Have the students repeat with you examples of this type of sandwich, as in the following exercises:

   Tengo que ir.   Tenemos que jugar.

   Tuve que salir.   Tuvieron que cerrar.

   Tenía que comer.   Teníamos que estudiar.

4. Place a filling of DE between the slices of another sandwich. Place several verbs using DE on top of the first piece of bread. Practice orally.

   Acabo de comer.   Acaban de chocar.

   Acabaste de verlo.   Acabaron de mirarlo.

   Terminé de trabajar.   Terminaron de estudiar.

   Trato de entenderlo.   Trataron de escapar.

5. Place another filling of A between the slices of another sandwich. List the verbs on top of the first piece of bread, then practice orally. Try to categorize for students the types of verbs that take A, such as movement, teaching, learning, and beginning.

   Vamos a salir.   Van a comer.

   Sales a tomar.   Vienen a comer.

   Empiezo a trabajar.   Comienzo a estudiar.

   Aprendo a leer.   Le enseño a tocarlo.

   Invito a comer.   Vuelven a dormir.

6. Continue with other combinations, if desired, before the diet sandwich is approached.

7. Now mention that if the top verbs do not take slices of A, DE, QUE, or any other filling, one must assume that they are "diet sandwiches," thus, nothing in the middle. Drill examples of common verbs with which students are already familiar.

Necesito dormir.	Puede ir.
Deben estudiar.	¿Sabes esquiar?
Quieren aprenderlo.	No queremos comer más.

8. Wipe off the top slice verbs. Drill using HACER as the second slice. As you give a top slice verb, students should repeat the top slice verb, the filling, and HACER, until you can ascertain whether students are guessing correctly. This can be done chorally or individually.

<u>Voy</u> (a hacer)	<u>Tienen</u> (que hacer)	<u>Acaban</u> (de hacer),
Tratan	Necesito	Puedo
Salimos	Tuvimos	Aprenden
Enseñan	No quiero	Vienes

9. If there is difficulty, refresh the memory of the students by pointing out the four different sandwiches, then by choosing an easier drill before reverting back to the more difficult one in Step 8. Step 9 is an easier drill that just requires students to provide the "filling."

Use the verbs in Step 8 but elicit only the filling. For example, as the teacher says "voy," the students should respond with "a," "tienen" with "que," "puedo" with "nothing" or "diet."

10. If desired, the teacher might choose to end with a translation drill. Individual students should be asked to volunteer rather than selecting students who might still stumble at this point.

I want to eat.	He needs to eat.	They have to eat.
We try to sing.	We learn to sing.	We need to sing.
He just saw.	He finished working.	He should work.
They come to eat.	They go to eat.	They can eat.

11. These drills should be repeated on subsequent days until students are verbally comfortable with the topic.

The "deli sandwich" idea is also conducive to the learning of French. Similar drills can easily be made up.

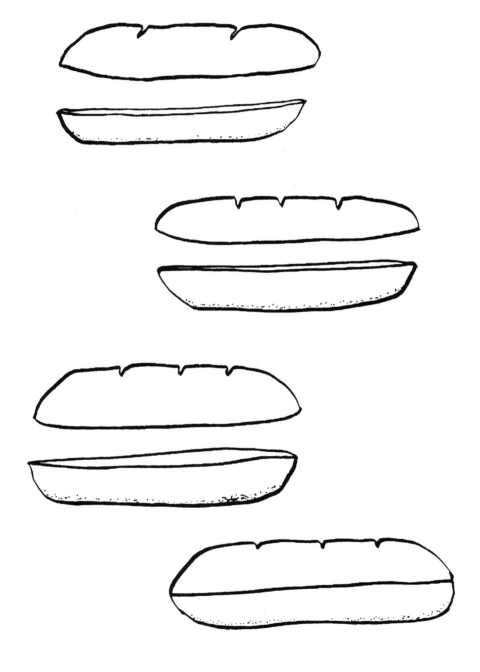

tener

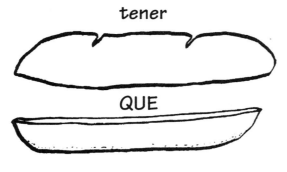

QUE

acabar, terminar, tratar

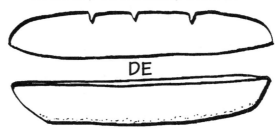

DE

ir, venir, empezar, enseñar, aprender, invitar

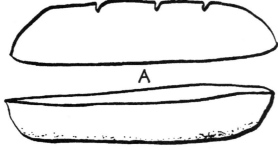

A

querer, necesitar, poder, saber

PREPOSITION STREETS: Prepositions and Prepositional Phrases

INTRODUCTION: Prepositions must be taught in a graphic or visual sense since they indicate the position of one word to another. Prepositional phrases at times require combining with the definite articles, or gender markers, a task that students find difficult to understand. Try presenting them as intersecting roads that come from two different directions.

PROCEDURE FOR TEACHING PREPOSITIONS

1. To instill meaning, cut out from a magazine a picture of an animal and one of a car or house; even better would be the use of actual miniatures of a car and an animal.

2. Place the animal *above, below, inside, next to, far from, close to, behind, in front of,* as well as *on* and *in* the house. Pronounce the preposition as the meaning is demonstrated. Students should listen for meaning and for pronunciation.

3. Have students demonstrate with the animal and car the various positions as enunciated: *above, below,* and so forth.

4. Now have the students pronounce the words with you as you again show the different positions of the animal to the house.

5. Place the animal in the various positions as the students call out the correct word for the appropriate preposition, without verbal prodding. When students have demonstrated a firm knowledge of meaning and good pronunciation, continue by expanding into prepositional phrases.

PROCEDURE FOR PREPOSITIONAL PHRASES

1. Review meanings of common prepositions.

2. Drill north to south road using a small toy car. Point out the male and female lanes of *en el teléfono, en la casa, entre el carro y* (any object). Drive the car from north to south as the prepositional phrases above are enunciated.

3. Now explain that the west-to-east street involves larger prepositions which combine with DE. Give a couple of examples: *lejos de, cerca de, detrás de, delante de, arriba de, al lado de.*

4. Using the car, move from west to east as you have students repeat with you some feminine examples:

   detrás de la casa, delante de la escuela, arriba de la goma, dentro de la casa, lejos de la silla, cerca de la casa, al lado de la goma.

   Point out that this is the feminine lane.

5. Using the car, move from west to east again as you have students repeat with you some examples from the masculine lane. Point out that instead of DE and EL you will be combining the two into DEL.

   detrás del carro, delante del carro, arriba del libro, lejos del parque, cerca del parque, al lado del banco, dentro del carro

6. Return to the north-to-south route and repeat the feminine and masculine examples. Remind students that there are no combinations here. Return to the west-to-east route and repeat the feminine and masculine examples.

7. Finally, try some mix-and-match exercises by using EL CARRO. Give students some prepositions for which they should provide the whole prepositional phrase.

   Examples of step 7:

GIVE	EXPECT
detrás	detrás del carro
en	en el carro
delante	delante del carro
entre	entre el carro y. . .
arriba	arriba del carro
cerca	cerca del carro

8. Check to make sure that students do not combine DE with feminine nouns.

GIVE	EXPECT
detrás, casa	detrás de la casa
detrás, carro	detrás del carro
delante, casa	delante de la casa
delante, carro	delante del carro

9. Check to make sure that students remember which prepositions use DE.

GIVE	EXPECT
en, casa	en la casa
en, carro	en el carro
cerca, casa	cerca de la casa
cerca, carro	cercal del carro

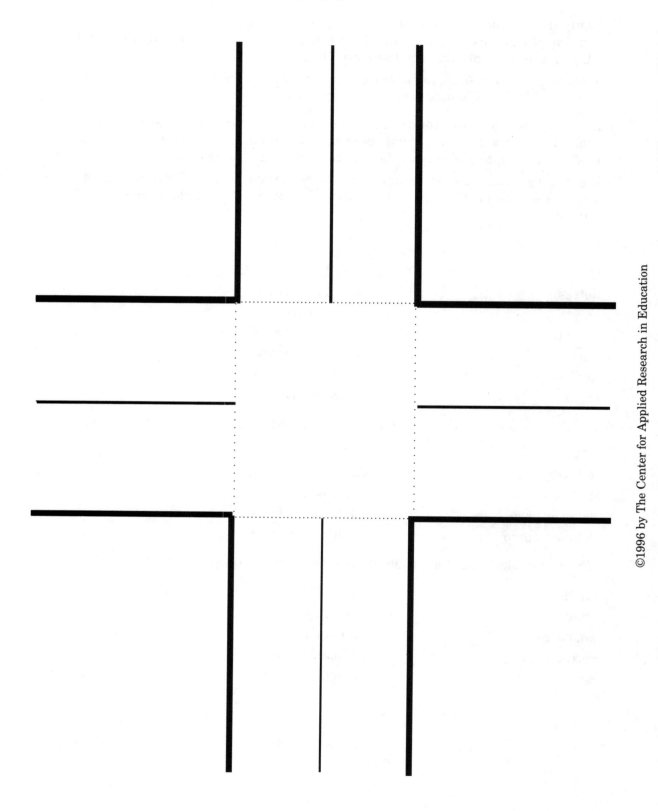

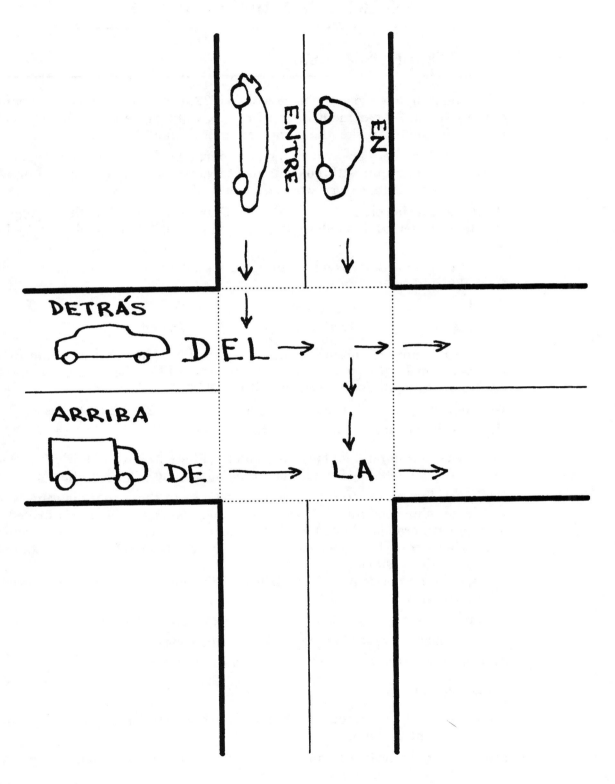

APARTMENTS: <u>Gustar</u>—To Like

HOW TO USE THE VISUAL DIAGRAM

1. Show the completed visual diagram of GUSTAR. Explain briefly the meaning of the structure. Apartment B, or column B, will translate as: I like, you like, he, she, you like, we like, they (and you, plural) like.

2. Point out that there are two rooms per apartment (column). Since this GUSTAR structure requires three columns of two rooms, you will be dealing with six rooms per sentence, one word per room.

3. Point out that in column B, GUSTA and GUSTAN will reflect their neighbors in column C. GUSTA is followed by EL and LA. GUSTAN is followed by LOS and LAS.

4. Isolating column B, focus on meaning. Ask students to find: he likes, we like, they like, and so on.

We like.	Do you like?	She likes.
He likes.	They like.	You (formal) like.

5. Put the meaning of column B together with the structures in column C by requesting in English such combinations as: He likes the house, We like the houses. Remind students to choose either GUSTA or GUSTAN.

We like the book.	I like the books.	She likes the book.
He likes the houses.	Do you like the house?	Do they like the book?

6. Now focus on column A for emphasis and for differentiation. Ask which areas in column A are necessary for differentiation (<u>él, ella, usted, ellos, ellas, ustedes</u>).

7. Drill each line across (columns A, B, and C) as in the visual diagram before you erase column B (only the pronouns). Once you have adequately drilled the pattern with pronouns, point out that proper names can be inserted in column A, or other alternatives such as los chicos, or mis abuelos. Give a few examples such as: *A Juan, Al chico* and so on.

   After the pronouns have been drilled, drill some alternatives to apartment A, or column A.

A Juan le gusta la casa.	A María le gustan los libros.
A mis amigos les gusta la casa.	A tus amigos les gusta la casa.
A la chica le gusta la casa.	*<u>Al</u> chico le gustan las casas.

   *This should be pointed out briefly.

8. After erasing the pronouns in column B, have the students replace them orally as you point to them.

9. Erase the pronouns in column A. Have the students replace them orally as you point to them (not necessarily in order).

10. Ask students for the whole concept from A to C by asking for such English concepts as: I really like the houses, They really like the book, and so forth.

I really like the house.	She really likes the house.
Juan really likes the book.	Juan really likes the books.
We really like the house.	We really like the houses.
María really likes the books.	María really likes the book.

11. Once the basic pattern has been solidified, point out the lightning bolt, which represents the negative NO. You may want to sketch in a bolt between columns A and B all the way down the line as the patterns are drilled orally using the sentences in the visual.

12. A few translations from English to drill the meaning with negatives may be done at this point.

María really doesn't like the book.	She really doesn't like the house.
I really don't like the house.	We really don't like the house.
Juan really doesn't like the books.	He really doesn't like the book.

13. Before all the pronouns are erased again, recap by asking some questions, for example:

   a. For this concept how many rooms need to be filled up?

   b. What word resides in the very first room in column A, and thus, is the very first word of the sentence?

   c. Where do you visualize the negative lightning bolt?

1-85

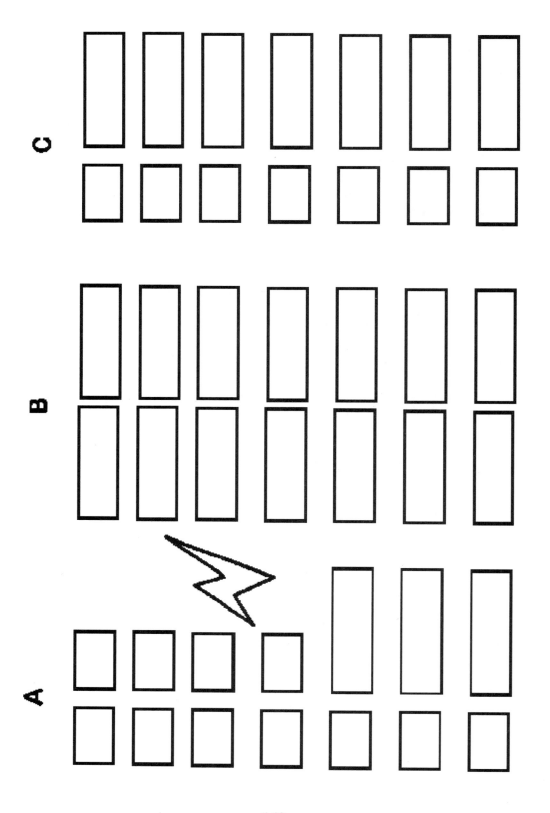

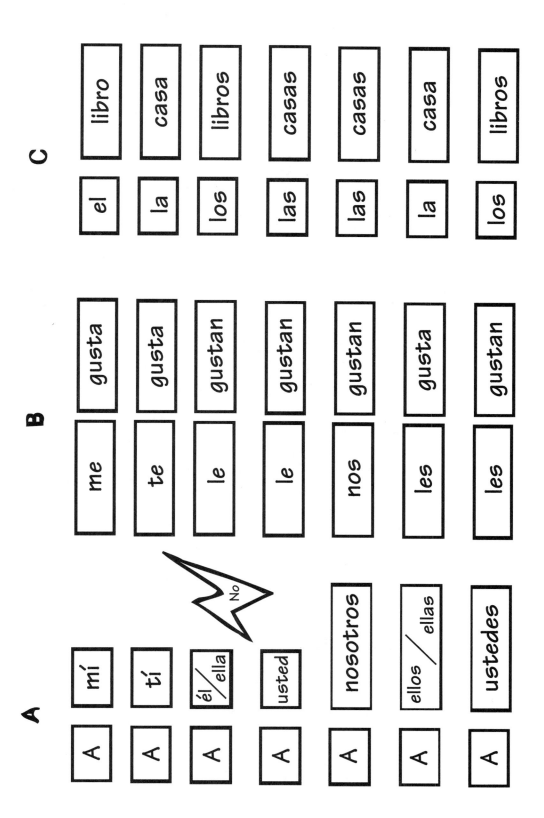

A

A — mí
A — tí
A — él/ella
A — usted
A — nosotros
A — ellos / ellas
A — ustedes

No

B

me gusta
te gusta
le gustan
le gustan
nos gustan
les gusta
les gustan

C

el libro
la casa
los libros
las casas
las casas
la casa
los libros

HEART: <u>Gustar</u>

INTRODUCTION: This activity offers a very visual way of establishing the meaning of the verb, as well as the structure. The happy heart will represent "liking" something. This works well when you are teaching younger children.

HOW TO USE THE VISUAL DIAGRAM

1. Ask students if they like chocolate. This will assist in engaging interest in presenting the verb.

2. In the smaller heart, place the word GUSTA, telling students the meaning, but that now you need to know *who* likes chocolate. On the line to the right, place the words EL CHOCOLATE, and below it LA CASA.

3. On the top line to the left of the heart, place <u>me</u>, then practice a couple of examples with students, such as:

   ME GUSTA EL CHOCOLATE.

   ME GUSTA LA CASA.

4. Fill in the "you" space with <u>te</u>, and have the students repeat the above sentences representing "You like . . . ."

5. Continue with "he," "she" and "you" (formal) by adding <u>le</u>, then by practicing the above two sentences.

6. Erase the pronouns, and ask the students how to say:

HE LIKES.	I LIKE.
SHE LIKES.	YOU LIKE (informal).
YOU LIKE.	DO YOU LIKE (formal)?

7. Proceed with "we," by adding "NOS," drill, then add "they" and "you" (plural), and drill. Point out that the verb does not change yet.

8. Erase all pronouns again, and have students replace them orally according to meaning.

9. Now it is time for negatives. Present the idea, "I don't like school." Show students that the word NO is placed in the diamond to the left of ME. Place NO in every diamond, then drill orally:

   NO ME GUSTA LA ESCUELA.

   NO TE GUSTA EL LIBRO.

   NO LE GUSTA LA ESCUELA.

   NO NOS GUSTA EL LIBRO.

   NO LES GUSTA LA ESCUELA.

10. Having erased everything, ask students the following meanings from the native language to the target language:

I LIKE THE BOOK.

WE DON'T LIKE THE BOOK.

THEY LIKE SCHOOL.

HE DOESN'T LIKE CHOCOLATE.

11. Now it is time for plurals. Ask a question such as, "Do you like asparagus?" Using the lines to the right of the big heart, place LOS ESPÁRRAGOS and LAS CASAS. Point out that "LOS" and "LAS" words, or any other plural indicators, require a larger heart called GUSTAN. Place GUSTAN in the center of the heart.

12. Ask students to recall all the pronouns on the left side. Pronounce together numerous examples of the plural, indicating with a pointer or finger, the trip from left to right:

ME	GUSTAN	LOS	ESPARRAGOS.
LE	GUSTAN	LAS	CASAS.
NOS	GUSTAN	LAS	CASAS.
¿TE	GUSTAN	LOS	ESPARRAGOS?

13. Repeat the above with NO.

14. To see if the students understand which size heart to use, small GUSTA or big GUSTAN, give them some new subjects for which they should call out "GUSTA" or "GUSTAN."

New subjects: los discos, el lápiz, los Estados Unidos, la blusa

15. Erase all information on the hearts, and ask students to formulate the following sentences, using diamonds, pronouns, and two different hearts:

I don't like asparagus.

We like records.

He likes records.

They like school.

She doesn't like the house.

Do you like the United States?

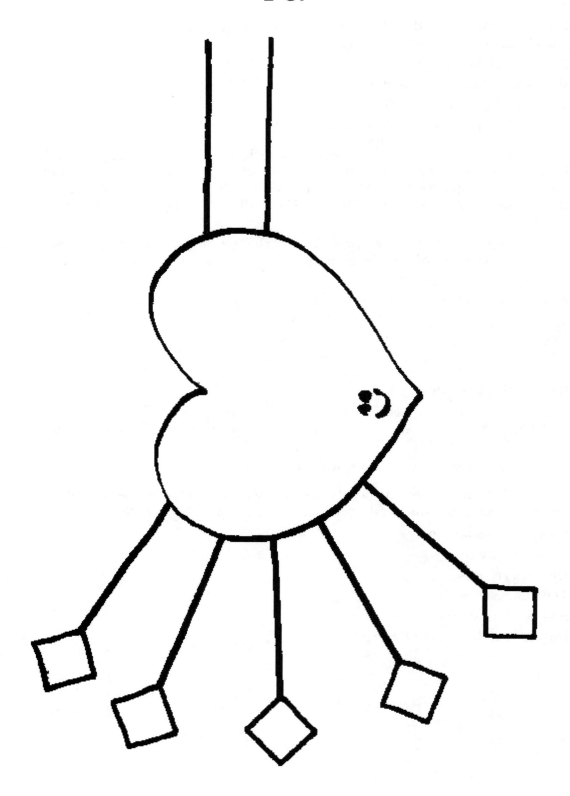

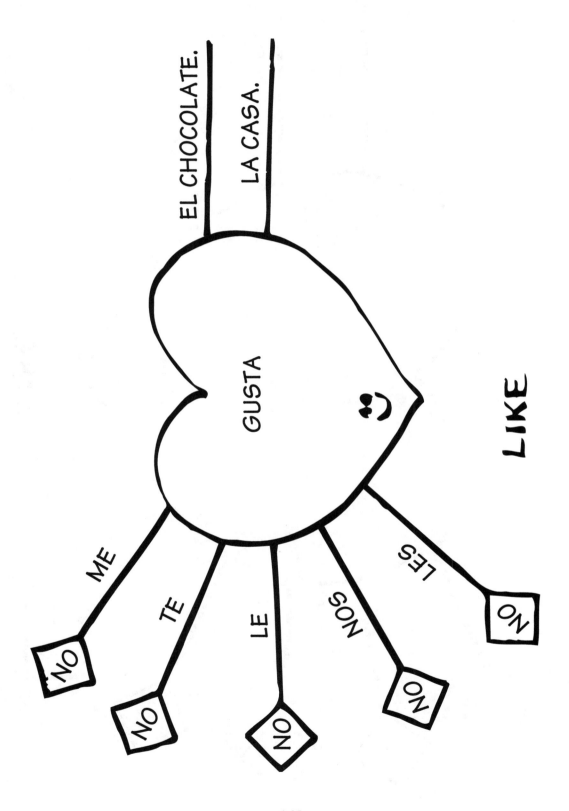

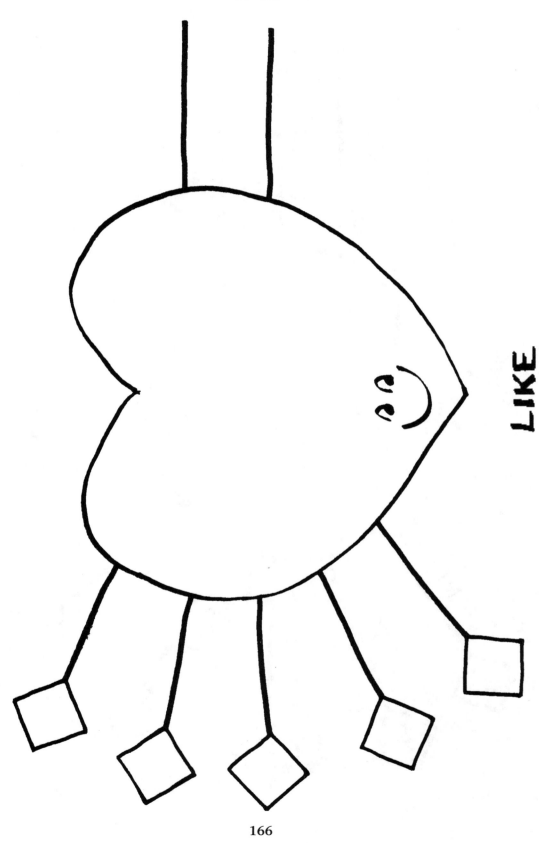

LIKE

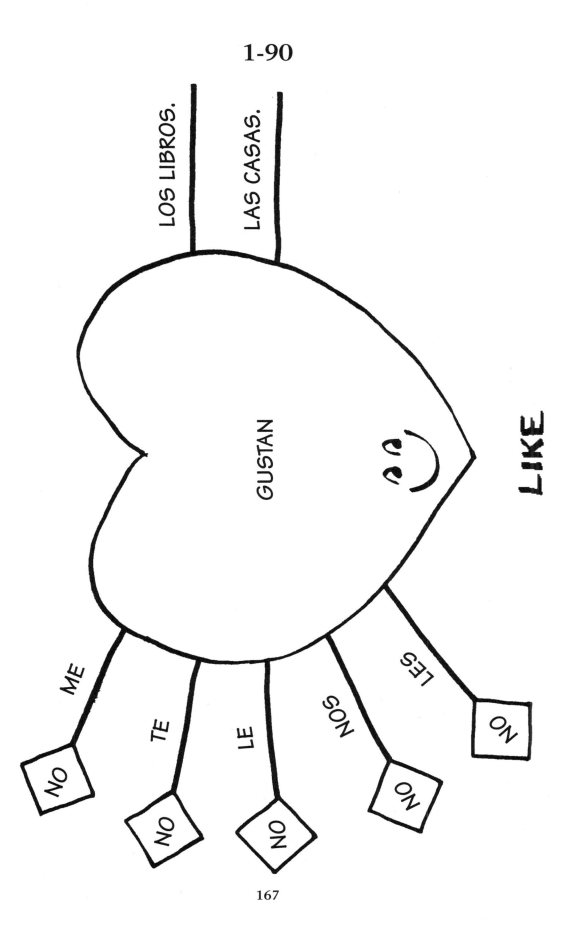

ROLL CALL: Gustar

INTRODUCTION: As a reinforcement of the GUSTAR concept, have students do a "Gustar Roll Call" on the days following the initial presentation of the concept.

PROCEDURE

1. Ask all students to stand up.
2. Explain that each person will contribute to a statement about liking something.
3. Have the first person say, "I like school." If the answer is correct, the student sits down. The student remains standing if the answer is incorrect. Choose a student who would probably guess correctly as the first respondent to model the sentence pattern.
4. Have the second student say, "You like school." Proceed as above.
5. The third student should say, "He likes school."
6. Once the "I like" through "They like" loop has been completed, begin the loop: "I like books." This drills the plural form of gustar.
7. Work the loop as indicated above from "I like books" through "They like books."
8. Return to the students who remain standing. To give them the chance to sit down, return to the loop: "I like school" through "They like school." If they listened to the other students who answered correctly, you'll hear more correct responses.
9. On subsequent days, start the roll call with a different student and a variation of gustar, such as, "I don't like school."

SWINGS: Comparatives of Inequality for Adjectives—Regular and Irregular

Prior to teaching the formation, give a few sentences in English to point out the -er than, more. . . than, and less. . . than constants in the comparative structure.

HOW TO USE THE VISUAL DIAGRAM

1. Write MAS along the left side of the first swing, ALTO (or any adjective) along the top, and QUE along the right side of the swing. (For French, write PLUS, JOLIE, and QUE along the same lines.) Explain that this is the regular comparative.

2. Drill several sentences with this model, as below:

   más alto que, José es más alto que Juan. Juan es más alto que Pablo.

   (plus jolie que, Elise est plus jolie que Marie. Marie est plus jolie que sa soeur.)

3. Use the second box to drill another alternative for plurals such as, MAS RICOS QUE. (For French use PLUS RICHES QUE.)

   más ricos que, Mis abuelos son más ricos que nosotros. Son más ricos que yo.

   (plus riches que) Mes grandparents sont plus riches que nous. Ils sont plus riches que moi.

4. Use one swing to show the MENOS. . . QUE (MOINS . . . QUE) structure, and drill these for form and meaning.

   menos alto que, Juan es menos alto que José. Pablo es menos alto que Juan.

   (moins riches que, Mes parents sont moins riches que mes grandparents. Je suis moins riche que mes grandparents.)

5. Try a few regular comparatives from the English translation standpoint.

richer than	less tall than	smarter than
less smart than	nicer than	less nice than

6. Begin the irregular comparatives by filling in the left arm of the collapsed swing with MEJOR and the right one with QUE, point out the meaning, and drill in a short sentence. (In French, place MEILLEUR QUE on the same lines.) Announce the new shape of a collapsed swing.

mejor que	Juan es mejor que yo.	Yo soy mejor que ella.
(meilleur que	Il est meilleur que moi.	Je suis meilleur que toi.)

7. Fill in the other three angles with: PEOR QUE, MAYOR QUE, and MENOR QUE. Point out the meaning, and drill in short sentences. (For French use only one angle for PIRE QUE.)

peor que	Yo soy peor que tú.	El es peor que yo.
(pire que	Il est pire que moi.	Je suis pire que toi.)
mayor que	Yo soy mayor que Juan.	Juan es mayor que Pablo.
menor que	Juan es menor que yo.	Pablo es menor que Juan.

8. From an English translation, check that the students know the meaning of the irregular comparatives.

worse than   older than   younger than   better than

9. Now mix up the regular and irregular comparatives and drill for form and meaning.

10. Recap by having the students focus on the visual diagram, and explain how the regular pattern is different from the irregular pattern (swing vs. the collapsed swing, MAS- (MENOS) for regular comparatives (PLUS and MOINS for French).

less rich than I	better than
nicer than I	blonder than
less happy than you	worse than
stricter than he	older than
more red than they	less red than
happier than we	younger than

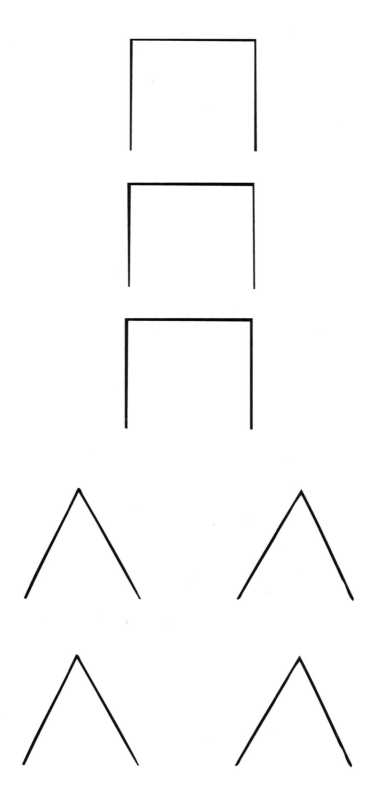

1-92

Regular:

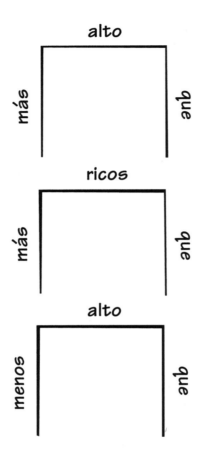

alto
más — que

ricos
más — que

alto
menos — que

Irregular:

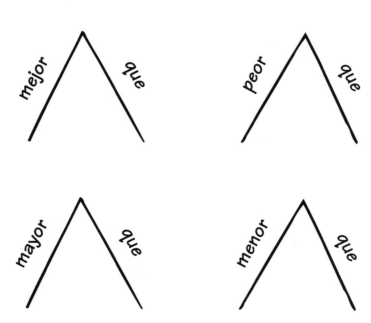

mejor que

peor que

mayor que

menor que

1-93

Regular:

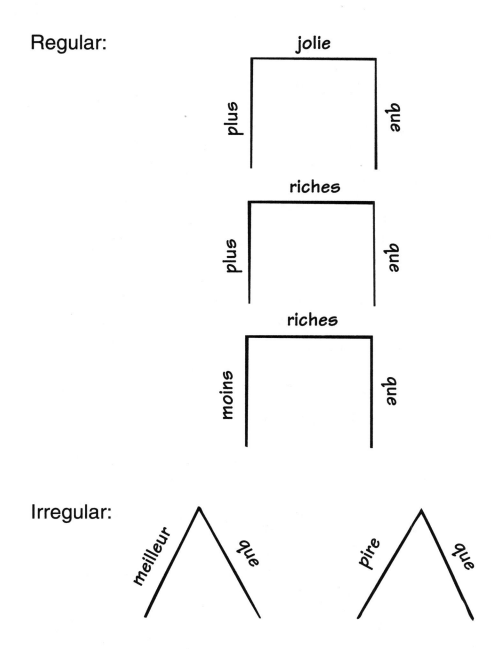

Irregular:

SIX-PACK AND FIVE-PACK: Regular Superlatives

INTRODUCTION: Since the irregular superlative structure follows the English pattern, only the regular superlative structure will be treated here. The visual diagram shows how the irregulars can be built onto the new model of six-packs and five-packs.

HOW TO USE THE VISUAL DIAGRAM

1. Draw six circles, as in the diagram, as if they were a six-pack of soda. Explain that each circle will represent a part of the regular superlative, for example: the most handsome boy in the class, the tallest girl on the team, the nicest teacher of all.

2. Placing one structure per circle, fill in with: EL, CHICO, MAS, ALTO, DE, TODO. Drill this orally, then try some other examples by pointing to the circle as each structure is enunciated. Try speeding up the phrases:

1.	2.	3.	4.	5.	6.
la	chica	más	alta	de	la clase
el	maestro	más	amable	de	la escuela
los	alumnos	más	ricos	de	la escuela

Practice some examples in which DE combines with EL:

el	jugador	más	fuerte	del	equipo
el	presidente	más	interesante	del	país

Practice some of the examples with MENOS in column 3 to express "the least."

3. Ask several conversation questions using this structure, for example:

   ¿Cómo se llama el chico más alto de la clase?

   ¿Cuál es el cereal más delicioso de todo?

   ¿Cuál es el actor más cómico?

4. When students are comfortable with the six-pack, refer back to the six-pack and remove the noun (circle 2) to form a five-pack. Ask students to repeat the same sentences with you, but without the noun. Try to speed up the phrases, then try them with MENOS instead of MAS:

la	más	alta	de	la clase
el	más	amable	de	la escuela
los	más	ricos	de	la escuela
el	más	fuerte	del	equipo
el	más	interesante	del	país

5. You may want to give some examples in English to see if the students have internalized the two different structures:

the most interesting book of all

the funniest of all

the most boring movie of all

the most intellectual of all

the least intellectual of all

6. If students have hesitated or made structural errors, repeat the examples until the patterns have been internalized.

7. The five- and four-pack designs are left in case you want to use them to teach the irregular structures. Because the irregulars do not cause a problem, they are not treated in this section.

1-94

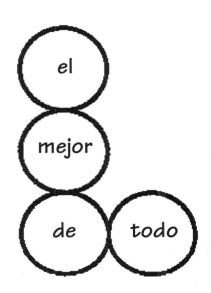

BARS: Pluralization

PURPOSE: To show students the extent of pluralization and to establish the concept that all related words are pluralized

INTRODUCTION: English-speaking students are used to pluralizing only the verb and the nouns. When learning a foreign language, they must often remember to pluralize almost every other part of speech.

PROCEDURE

For French:

1. Fill in each box with a word from a singular sentence using definite articles (instead of indefinite articles), as in the diagram. LE LIVRE EST BLANC.

2. Tell students that all related words become pluralized. Some involve sound changes; some don't, but all involve written changes.

3. Ask students to listen for the number of sound changes as you pluralize the sentence. LES LIVRES SONT BLANCS.

4. When students respond with "two changes," write the plural in the plural bars, requesting that students note how many written changes there are. Students should respond with "four changes."

5. Try the same procedure with a feminine sentence. LA MAISON EST BLANCHE. Write the feminine form in the singular bar. Then orally pluralize to elicit from students the fact that there are two oral or audible changes.

6. Write the plural sentence in the plural bars, then ask how many written or visual changes there are.

7. Give students some more examples of singular sentences by writing the simple sentences in the bars, then by having students orally pluralize the sentences while a volunteer writes the sentences either at the blackboard or on the overhead.

   Sample sentences: LE MAGASIN EST OUVERT.

   LA VOITURE EST BLEUE.

   LA VALISE EST FERMEE.

8. Wrap up by asking students to recall the important point about pluralizing: <u>All related words become pluralized</u>. This should be followed up by a written activity so that all students have practice with the concept.

   Comment: While this topic is more complex when it involves the whole spectrum of adjective agreements, agreement with indefinite articles, or any other gender markers, and liaison before vowels, only one basic concept is intended here—that of establishing that pluralization involves more than just the verb and noun.

For Spanish:

1. Write a simple sentence with one word per space in the bars indicated in the diagrams. Use definite articles. EL LIBRO ES BLANCO.

2. Tell students that when pluralizing, all words become pluralized, not just the verb and noun. Ask students to listen for the four changes as you enunciate the plural sentence while pointing to each block of the bars.

3. Write the plural sentence in the plural bars. Circle the radically different changes from EL to LOS and from ES to SON.

4. Try the same procedure with a feminine sentence. LA CASA ES BLANCA. After writing in the singular sentence, ask students how many changes are made in the plural. Enunciate the plural sentence.

5. When the students say "four changes," write the sentence in the plural bars, circling the radical verb change of ES to SON. Stress the point that everything does become pluralized.

6. Experiment with some more samples by writing the singular sentences in the bars, then by having students orally pluralize them while a student writes the plural at the board or overhead.

   Sample sentences: EL SACO ES NEGRO.

                           LA BLUSA ES ROJA.

                           EL CHICO ES ALTO.

7. Wrap up by asking students to recall the important point about pluralizing: All related words become pluralized. This should be followed up by a written activity so that all students have practice with the concept.

   Comment: This topic is much more complex since it involves the many facets of agreement. Only one basic concept is being stressed here—the general, but new concept of pluralizing everything. Once the students have indicated an awareness of this concept, you can proceed with all the other ramifications.

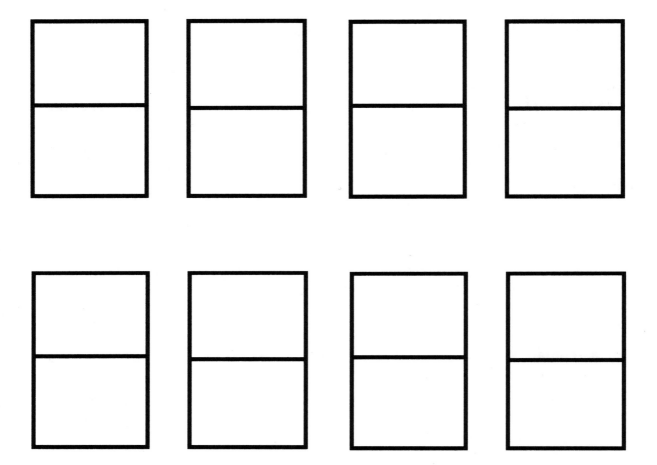

SINGULAR SENTENCE:

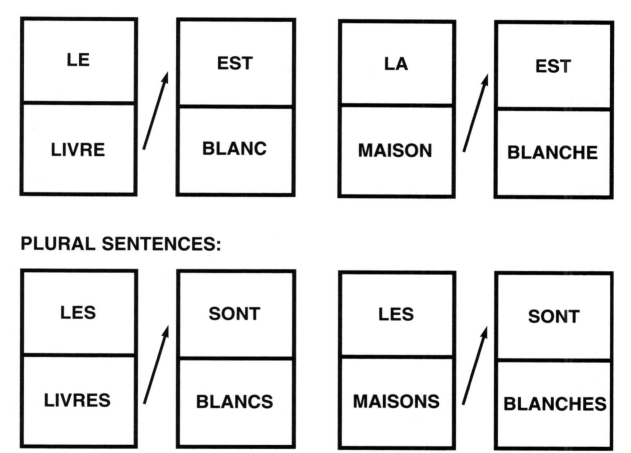

PLURAL SENTENCES:

SINGULAR SENTENCE:

EL	ES		LA	ES
LIBRO	BLANCO.		CASA	BLANCA.

PLURAL SENTENCES:

LOS	SON		LAS	SON
LIBROS	BLANCOS		CASAS	BLANCAS

DOUGHNUT: Por vs. Para

INTRODUCTION: This topic must be reduced to the simplest explanation the first time around. Once students grasp the main differences between the two words, they can expand their understanding of it.

HOW TO USE THE VISUAL DIAGRAM

1. In the center of the doughnut, place the words DESTINATION in the right half, and PURPOSE in the left half. Both are reasons to use PARA. Write PARA across the top of the doughnut hole, as in the visual.

2. Before orally drilling some examples with the class, point out that PURPOSE is usually used with verbs.

    DRILL:

    para vivir   un vaso para beber

    para comer   para escribir su nombre

3. Point out that DESTINATION could refer to people, places, things, and times, as in a specific due date, the "destination" time.

    DRILL:

    people: para mí   para ella   para mi hermana
    places: Van para Miami.   Salen para San Diego.
    things: para el periódico   el artículo para el periódico
                para la puerta   la llave para la puerta
    times: para mañana   para la semana próxima
                para hoy   para el mes que viene

4. Explain that POR has many different meanings. Write POR across the top of the circle, then write IN EXCHANGE FOR in the doughnut, then PER, IN, FOR, THROUGH, ALONG, and BY scattered around the doughnut. Refer to the completed visual diagram if needed.

5. Drill each definition around the doughnut.

    DRILL:

    in exchange for: por dos dólares   por diez pesos
    per: por docena   por semana
    in: (a general time)   por la mañana   por la tarde
    for: (duration of time) por tres años   por una semana
    through: por el bosque   por el parque
    along: por el río   por la orilla

by: por correo   por teléfono
                              por avión   por coche

6. With the chart in front of the students, give some obvious verbal clues for which the students should guess POR or PARA, then repeat the whole phrase as a group with them. Try to avoid clues that could be both POR and PARA. For example, given the clue "Miami" students would not know if one is en route to Miami or just passing through.

CLUES:

GIVE	REPEAT
mañana	para mañana
docena	por docena
la noche	por la noche
teléfono	por teléfono
comer	para comer
la semana próxima	para la semana próxima
vivir	para vivir
tres años	por tres años
la mañana	por la mañana

7. You may wish to try a drill with English clues:

GIVE	EXPECT
by mail	por correo
in order to eat	para comer
through the forest	por el bosque
per month	por mes
in order to enter	para entrar
headed for Los Angeles	para Los Angeles
by plane	por avión
for the newspaper	para el periodico
for us	para nosotros
for ten years	por tres años

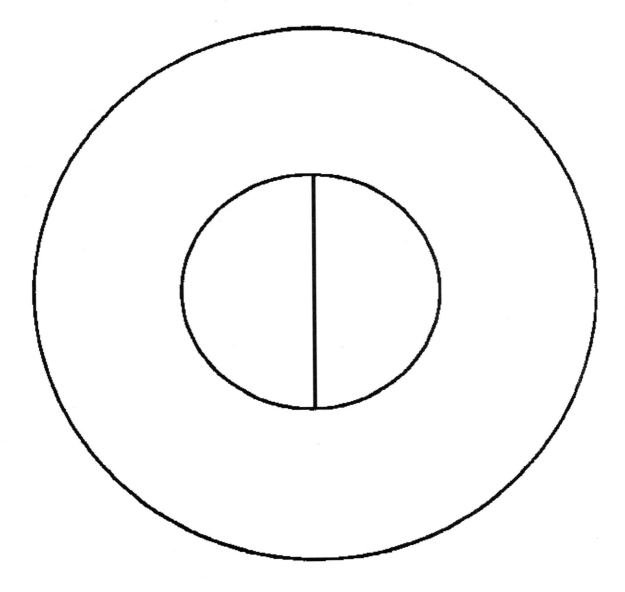

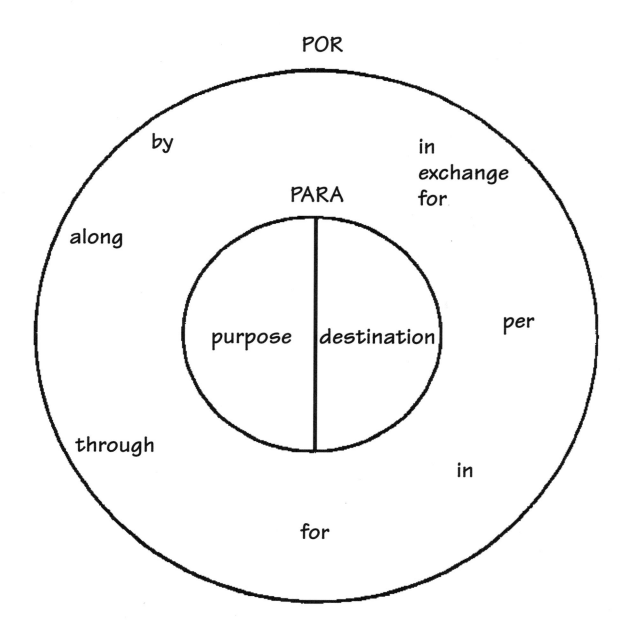

POR

by

in
exchange
for

PARA

along

per

purpose | destination

through

in

for

DOUGHNUT: Ser vs. Estar

INTRODUCTION: Teachers know how difficult this concept is for students. A frequent question is, "What's the difference between ser and estar?" Students admit that they never really understood the explanations. For some reason, they tend to overuse estar. As with the por vs. para concept, a "brief-and-to-the-point" approach is taken to establish the most obvious differences between ser and estar.

HOW TO USE THE VISUAL DIAGRAM

1. In the small center circle there should be a dividing line to separate two important words. On the left, write LOCATION. On the right, write CONDITION (or state). Place ESTA on top of the circle, as in the visual diagram.

2. Explain to the students that forms of ESTAR will be used to indicate location, then have students repeat several examples with you.

DRILL:

Está en casa.	Está en el carro.	Está arriba.
¿Dónde están?	Está aquí.	Está cerca.

3. Explain that forms of ESTAR will be used to indicate condition, or a state, such as being sick, well, tired, nervous, happy, furious, or absent, then drill several examples with the students.

DRILL:

Está enfermo.	¿Cómo está?	Está sentado.
Están bien.	Estamos mal.	Está nervioso.
Estoy preocupado.	Estoy contento.	Está triste.
Está en el centro.	Están a la derecha.	Están allí.

4. Because there are many reasons for the use of SER you should choose how many, and which ones, should be taught the first time these differences are presented. Those reasons should be placed in the doughnut, followed by separate drills for each use. Students should be made aware of some non-state or non-condition situations. Samples of some are included below:

DRILL:

General description or identification:	Es alto.	Eres amable.
	Son americanos.	Es médico.
	Somos estudiantes.	Soy profesora.
	Son guapos.	Es verde.
	Son azules.	Es mi hermano.

	¿Quién es?	¿Cómo son?
	Es lunes.	¿Qué día es?
Origin:	Es de Perú.	Somos de aquí.
	Son de Puerto Rico.	Soy de Miami.

(Point out the key word DE to indicate origin.)

5. A contrastive drill of <u>ser</u> vs. <u>estar</u> is in order at this point. Give clues to the students, who should respond with <u>es</u> or <u>está</u>. Once the answer is guessed correctly, repeat the whole phrase with the students.

   CLUES:

GIVE	REPEAT
enfermo	Está enfermo.
simpático	Es simpático.
de San Juan	Es de San Juan.
bien	Está bien.
a la derecha	Está a la derecha.
furioso	Está furioso.
contento	Está contento.
alto	Es alto.
martes	Es martes.
italiano	Es italiano.
de Italia	Es de Italia.
profesor	Es profesor.
lejos	Está lejos.

6. Some translations from English might be given to some student volunteers.

GIVE	EXPECT
He is here.	Está aquí.
He is nice.	Es amable.
He is my friend.	Es mi amigo.
He is sick.	Está enfermo.
He is downstairs.	Está abajo.
He is American.	Es americano.

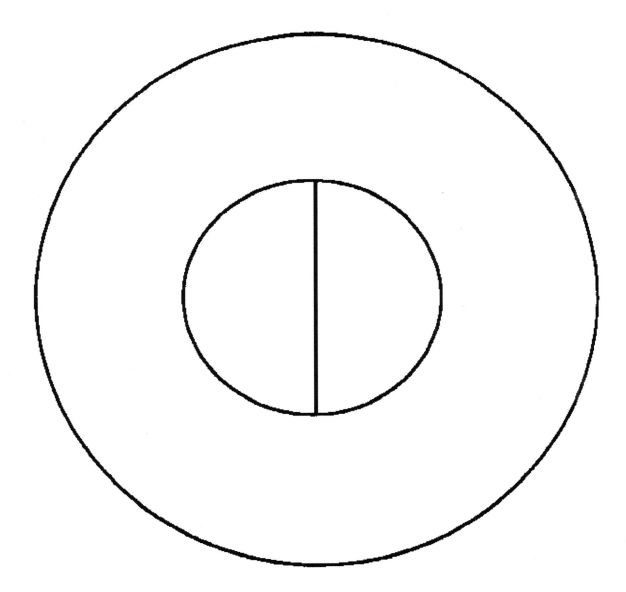

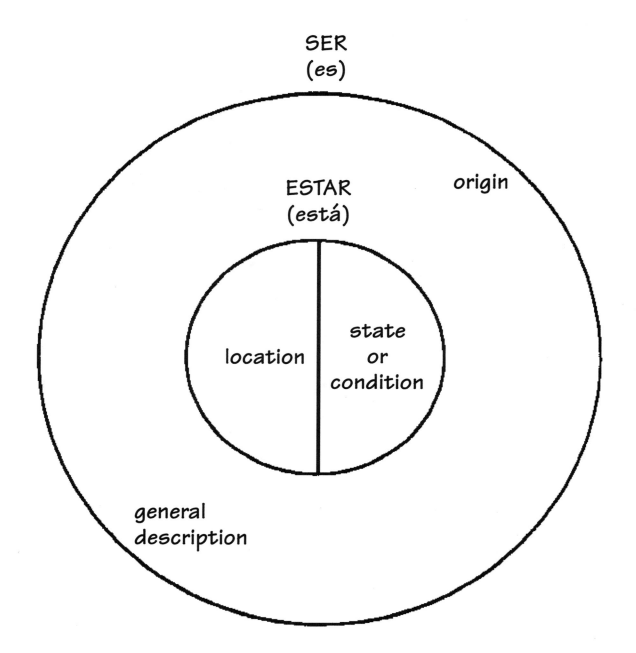

BOX: Ser vs. Estar

In keeping with a minimalist approach toward the teaching of grammar, the box enables students to focus on the most basic or important roles to learn. Once the basic concept has been grasped, the lesser used rules can be taught. The Functional-Notional approach to language learning has made us aware that not all rules need to be learned at once. This causes us to follow a certain hierarchy in terms of grammar rules with respect to their frequency in language use.

HOW TO USE THE VISUAL DIAGRAM

1. Draw four empty boxes (or squares) as in the visual diagram.

2. On the ESTAR side, fill in EN, and announce that this will be followed by expressions of location. Drill as follows:

   Está en casa.   Estoy en clase.   Están en la escuela.

   Estamos en Madrid.   Estoy en San Juan.   Estás en los Estados Unidos

3. Underneath the EN box, write in CONDITION or STATE and give some English expressions of temporary conditions. Drill these expressions in the foreign language.

   Estoy enfermo.   ¿Estás bien?   Están mal.

   Están sentados.   Estamos cansados.   Estoy nervioso.

4. In the top right box, write DE, and announce that it will be followed by places to indicate origin. Drill these.

   Soy de Nueva York.   ¿Eres de aquí?   Son de San Juan.

   Somos de allá.   Son de México.   Soy de los Estados Unidos.

5. In the bottom right box, write in GENERAL DESCRIPTION, and give some English expressions of general descriptions, such as, "I am tall," "They are blond." Drill these in the foreign language.

   Soy alto.   Eres bajo.   Son rubios.

   Somos ricos.   Son negros.   Soy morena.

   El es inteligente.   El perro es tonto.   Ella es cómica.

6. Before giving students added drills on the topic, erase the four cue ideas in the boxes. Ask students to orally replace the words just erased. Always keep the original answers in their own box as a stable point of reference.

ESTAR	SER
EN	DE
condition or state	general description

BOX: Saber vs. Conocer (Savoir vs. Connaître)

As explained in the previous example of a box, the need to provide a minimalist approach toward grammar rules, highlighting a hierarchy of most important rules for use, is answered by the use of a box for the two most important rules used to separate one verb from the other. Once the basics have been grasped, the other rules can be taught.

HOW TO USE THE VISUAL DIAGRAM

1. Draw four boxes as in the visual diagram, label with the verbs as headlines, and draw in the word FACT in the top left box.

2. After drawing some cue words, drill sentences with SABER (SAVOIR), as follows: Point out the question words of QUE, QUIEN, DONDE.

   ¿Sabes qué?   No sé dónde está.   No sé cuál quiere.

   Saben adónde voy.   ¿Sabes cuándo viene?   Sabemos quién gritó.

   (Tu sais où?   Je ne sais pas pourquoi.)

   (Nous ne savons pas combien.   Ils ne savent pas quand il se couche.)

   (Il sait que c'est vrai.   Elle sait qui l'a fait)

3. Underneath the first box, write in VERB, and drill sentences with SABER (SAVOIR).

   ¿Sabes nadar?   Yo sé esquiar.   No saben cocinar.

   ¿Sabemos patinar.   ¿Sabes jugar?   Yo no sé leer.

   (Tu sais nager?   Je ne sais pas lire.   On sait écrire.)

   (Vous savez le faire?   Nous savons skier.   Ils savent jouer.)

4. In the top right box, draw a face or faces to represent all people. Drill sentences with CONOCER (CONNAITRE).

   ¿Conoces a María?   ¿Conoces a Juan?   Conozco a la chica.

   Conocemos al grupo.   Conocen a mis amigos.   ¿Me conoces?

   (Tu connais mon amie? Je connais ton ami. Tu me connais?)

   (Ils connaissent mes amis. Nous les connaissons bien. Je le connais.)

5. In the bottom right draw the outline of a city to represent all places. Drill sentences with CONOCER (CONNAITRE).

   Conozco la ciudad.   ¿Conoces la calle?

   Conocen la capital.   No conocen España.

   (Je connais la ville.   Tu connais la rue?)

   (Ils connaissent le centre.   Nous connaissons Paris.)

6. Pointing to the box from which some contrastive sentences will be drilled, have students repeat teacher directed sentences.

Yo sé quién es.	Conozco a la chica.
Sé cómo se llama.	Conozco a María.
¿Sabes dónde está?	¿Conoces la ciudad?
¿Sabes adónde va?	¿Conoces el centro?
¿Sabes que va a Perú?	¿Conoces Perú?
Ella no sabe dónde vive.	Mama conoce a mi amigo.

(Je sais qui c'est.	Je connais la jeune fille.)
(Je sais comment elle s'appelle.	Je connais Marie.)
(Tu sais où il est?	Tu connais la ville?)
(Tu sais où il va?	Tu connais le centre?)
(Tu sais qu'il va à Paris?	Tu connais Paris?)
(Elle ne sait pas où il habite.)	Maman connaît mon ami.)

7. Erase everything from the boxes, and elicit from the students which key words or ideas were in the four boxes. Place their answers exactly in the original box. The placement of the answers must be standardized in this way.

SABER **facts** • qué • por qué • quién • adónde • dónde • cuál	**CONOCER** **people** 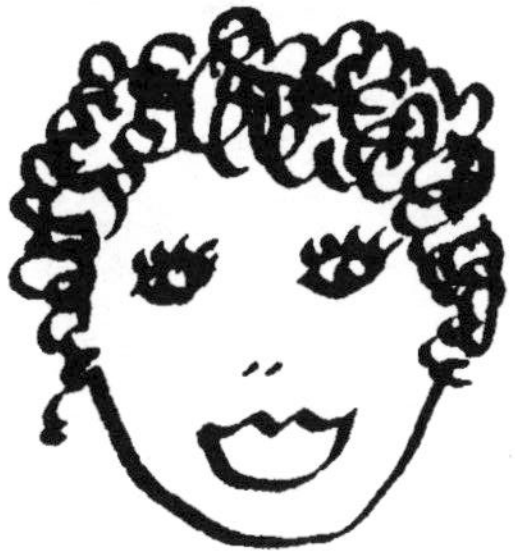 a la señorita
verb patinar	**places** 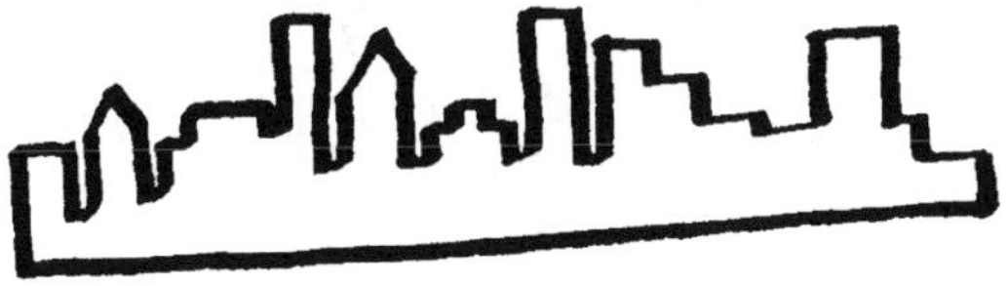 la ciudad

1-106

CONNAÎTRE	places
people la fille	 la ville
SAVOIR facts • où • lequel • qui • combien • pourquoi	verb patiner

©1996 by The Center for Applied Research in Education

TREBLE CLEF: Auditory Reinforcement

Music, with its melody and rhythm, serves as a powerful tool for learning and for retention of what has been presented. Jazz chants and rap have enhanced the scope of the use of music in teaching a concept. Math teachers have been known to teach geometry axioms and corollaries with rap techniques. Language teachers, too, can teach a syntactical structure, a sentence pattern, even vocabulary by superimposing the new material onto a well-known ditty, (such as "Row, Row, Row Your Boat," the first four notes of "Frere Jacques," the notes of "E-I-E-I-O" from "The Farmer in the Dell," etc.) or onto an easy rhythm. A whole host of material can be presented in this manner. It is a challenge to the creative nature of the instructor as to how extensively this can be used.

HOW TO USE THE VISUAL DIAGRAM

A treble clef may be drawn on the board, or use the transparency master, with the important notes blackened in so that students will see and hear the intonation of what is to be learned. Often we find that our students approach a foreign language with a monotone, so this may help—especially in the presentation of verb tenses—where it is the intonation or stress that indicates the tense or mood. In the visual diagram, an example shows the tone difference between the present and the preterit tense and the formal command vs. the preterit.

An example of a superimposed ditty and a grammar concept would be the tune "E-I-E-I-O" after which you would sing "Il me l'a donné." You could then substitute another example of "Je te l'ai donné" to the same tune of "E-I-E-I-O." Students would repeat the sentence according to the song.

An example of a superimposed rhythm as applied to a sentence pattern—such as the Spanish "Hace una hora que él llegó"—would be the use of a treble clef, onto which the corresponding notes are drawn and tapped out, or just tapped out. To tap out this sentence pattern, tap and say: <u>da da da da DA da da DA da da</u>, which corresponds to

<u>Ha ce un a hor a que él lle gó</u>.

Follow this with a slight change—that of a verb—by tapping with the fingers, or pointing to the "da da" words or notes on the treble clef, and saying: HACE UNA HORA QUE EL ENTRO. The students should follow you by saying the new sentence according to the "da da" rhythm. You can now change the subject of the verb as in: HACE UNA HORA QUE YO LLEGUE. Other changes could include the time period, as in: HACE DOS ANOS QUE YO LLEGUE. Try to find other linguistic patterns that fit, such as: HACE DOS ANOS QUE LO MIRO. (Point out that the subject has been dropped to accommodate the object pronoun.)

Now that you have established the sentence pattern via the rhythm, the challenge can be given to the students to volunteer a sentence that all students will repeat together according to the same rhythm.

The sentence pattern just described uses a rhythm that was conducive to a fun-filled drill in one of my Spanish I classes. The students were all willing to form a conga line around the periphery of the class, following me. We walked out the rhythm as if it were a dance. The right foot forward represented HA. The left foot forward represented CE, and so forth, until the whole pattern was walked out, accompanied by lots of giggles. Drop out of the leadership and move to the end of the line, so that a student may take the leadership to walk out the rhythm.

Finally, to help with the pronunication of a multisyllable word in the foreign language, the four notes of "Frère Jacques" can be hummed or sung, after which you split the syllables of the difficult word and sing it according to the song. For example, you might sing MAN TE QUI LLA, or IZ QUI ER DA. The students would follow you by repeating the word as a song.

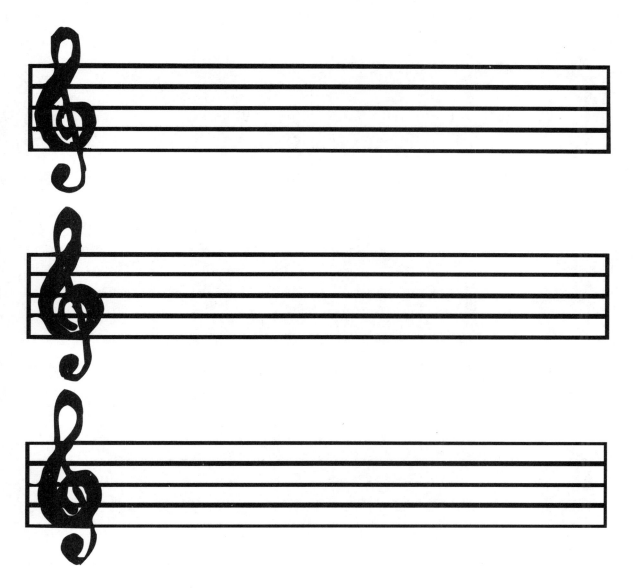

1-109

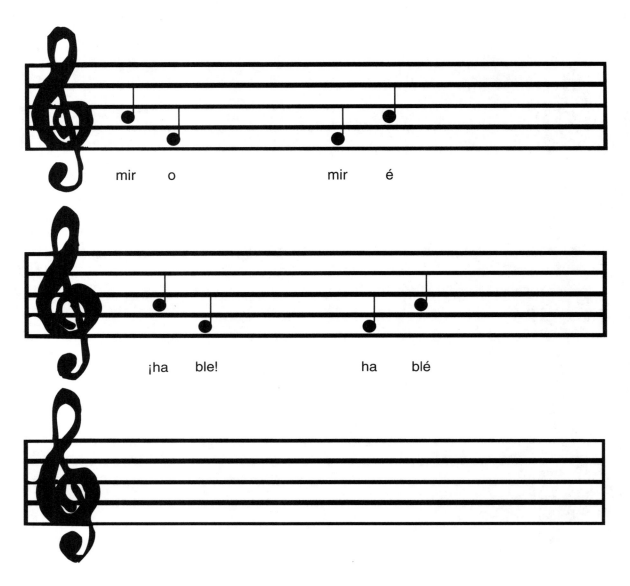

mir   o   mir   é

¡ha   ble!   ha   blé

MURAL LEARNING: For Review

INTRODUCTION: On those hot, sultry days when students can barely sit in their seats, when teaching and learning become a near impossibility, here's a cool suggestion that can be done with the lights dimmed, or off, in the case of bright sunlight. Many different grammar topics, recently taught or in need of review, can be displayed on the wall as described below. Also, prior to exams, when all learned material must be reviewed, this activity offers an alternative to providing volumes of review sheets.

PROCEDURE

1. Prepare one sample sentence of the target grammatical concept by writing it in big letters on a colored piece of paper. If the new concept is on <u>Reflexives</u>, then write a reflexive sentence such as <u>She gets up</u>, or <u>She gets angry</u>. Pastels (used for the copier machines) seem to be cooler in the hot weather.

2. Prepare other such sample sentences, one per piece of paper until you have a workable number, such as ten. This assignment is conducive to contrastive topics, such as object pronouns (direct, indirect, reflexive).

3. Number each paper at the top, then post on the walls, windows, and doors, with masking tape. The numbers should be mixed up—that is, not in chronological order, thus giving the impression of a treasure hunt. There should be a big distance between posted sentences so that the students don't have to crowd together.

4. Instruct students to leave their seats with pen and paper in hand. They should circulate around the room until they have found and written out the answers to all items on the sample papers. As always, some students will finish first. They can then help those who need it, or they can do textbook exercises at their desk, or consult their textbooks for the correct answers.

5. Once all students have sat down, or when you determine that it is time to begin the corrections, stand by each sentence, in chronological order, and ask a volunteer to give the answer to the first sentence. Another student should volunteer for the second, and so forth.

6. Students are to make corrections on their own papers, and ask questions pertaining to each numbered sentence before moving to the next number.

7. At the end of the correction session, the students can better quantify how many sentences they had incorrectly answered. They could put into two piles the correct vs. the incorrect sentences. A homework assignment might be to rewrite each sentence correctly into the notebooks.

An exciting aspect of this type of drill is that the students who have bunched up together at one sentence try to help one another with the answer. This presents an opportunity for cooperative learning.

Another benefit of this drill is the fact that students can more accurately determine how well they know the topic presented, so they know what to ask. For example, students have said, "I don't get the sentence on the door," "I don't get the sentence on the blue paper," and "How is the sentence on the first window different from the sentence on the third window?"

No matter what topic is drilled in this manner, the approach will enable students to be more active not only in their own learning, but also in the learning of their classmates, with the added benefit of a change of pace as they stand up for much of the class period.

vocabulary

grammar

CHAPTER SUMMARIES

cultural notes

idiomatic expressions

CITYSCAPE: Chapter Summary

Any configuration of city buildings can be used to summarize the concepts in each unit. One word or one verb ending should be placed in each building.

HOW TO USE THE VISUAL DIAGRAM

1. With the answers already written in each box, ask the students to find certain combinations that are printed before them as well as others based on the models—as in the exercises below.

   In Diagram:

   He likes football.   I like to play.

   Do you like to play?   Does she like to play?

   Based on Model:

   I like to swim.   Do you like to swim?

2. When students can do this successfully, erase the answers of this first concept. Now ask the same questions as in Step 1.

   What color is it?   What color is your car?

   What color is the house?   What color is the book?

3. For concept 2 (¿De qué color es. . .?) drill a few questions from translation, before you erase and ask the same questions.

4. For concept 3 give a verb to work with, such as llamar. Ask the students to form certain subject and verb combinations, first by giving only a subject.

   Using llamar:

usted	tú	ustedes	tú y yo
yo	él	él y yo	ellos

5. Once students can recognize which endings go with the subjects, then give the prompters by translation.

I call.	She calls.	We call.
They call.	Do you call?	My friend calls.

6. Now erase the endings and briefly repeat the previous exercises.

7. For concept 4, ask the students to locate the verb that matches your translation, such as: He plays, they play, and so on.

They play.	We play.	I play.
Does he play?	You play.	She plays.

(If question words have been learned, you can insert question words such as: when, what, why don't, where.)

8. Erase the endings and drill again.

9. Review either by asking the students to replace the words in each box or by repeating a mixture of sentences.

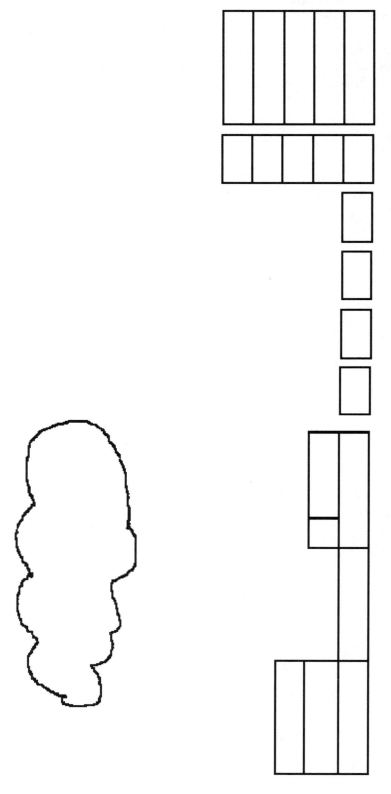

1-111

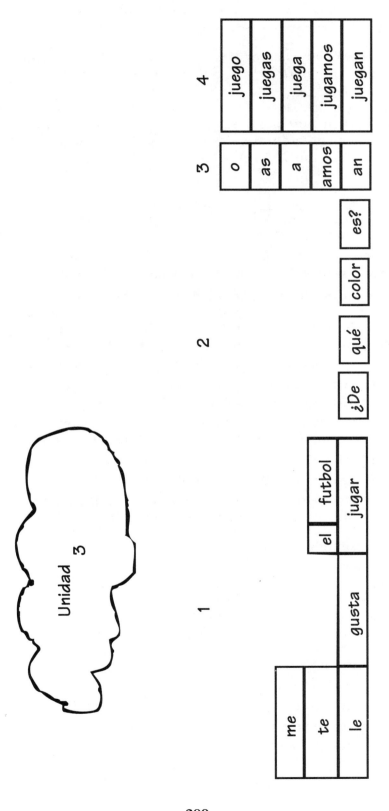

Unidad 3

1   2   3   4

3	4
o	juego
as	juegas
a	juega
amos	jugamos
an	juegan

¿De · qué · color · es?

| el | futbol |
| jugar |

| me |
| te |
| le |

gusta

MONSTER FACE: Chapter Summary

The particular chapter demonstrated on the visual diagram consists of four grammatical concepts (subject pronouns, regular verb conjugations and one irregular one in Spanish, <u>gustar</u>, and finally the concept of one possessive in a conversational context). It also has several categories of vocabulary. The more weird the monster face, the more memorable the image is to the students, and the more engaging it is in attracting their attention. The face should be constructed to accommodate the number of points taught in the chapter.

HOW TO USE THE VISUAL DIAGRAM

1. One concept should be plotted along the strands of hair. Point to the various strands, making sure that the basic subject pronouns have been learned.

2. The second concept is plotted around the eye on the left. Work from the inner eye to the second circle, then the third, until all the basic verbs in the chapter have been learned. If this is used for Spanish, the exception (I LIKE) should be pointed out and indicated with a big star next to it.

3. Proceed to the right eye and drill the concept of MY along with the proper syntax of noun and adjective. Remember to point out each word so as to train the students' vision and attention to the concept or word.

4. Point to the nose, starting either from the top or bottom, and elicit the vocabulary in order. Then mix up the words until no wrong answers are being given.

5. Proceed to the mouth, starting at the left or right, and elicit the vocabulary in order. Then mix up the words as in Step 4.

6. Erase everything on the monster face. Change the subject pronouns in the left eye and elicit a mixture of new combinations.

   For example:

He works.	They play.	We need.
Do you play?	Do you (plural) need?	She plays.

7. With everything erased, point to anywhere on the face and ask the students to respond in the foreign language according to the English prompter.

   For example:

They work at times.	I play often.
He plays always.	My favorite color . . .
My favorite pastime . . .	I never need the boots.
You always need the glove.	We need the court.

1-112

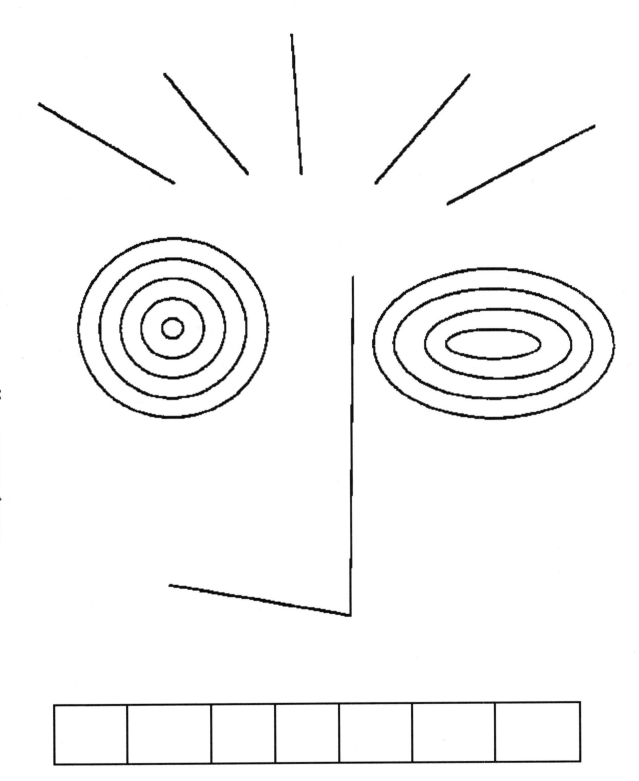

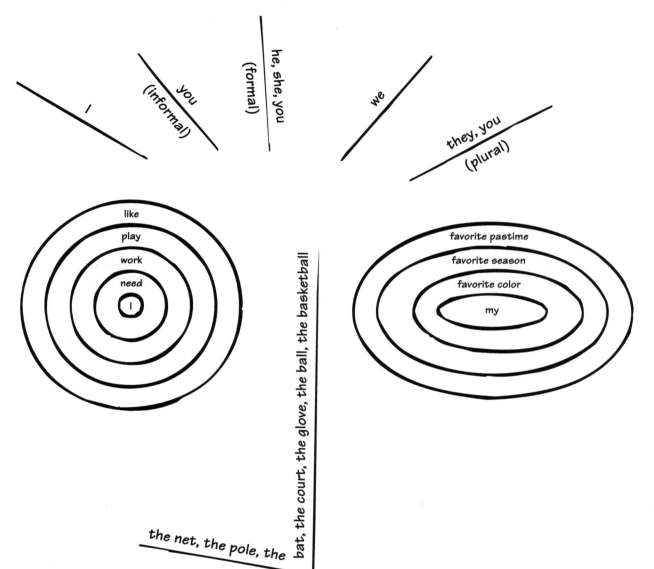

I

you (informal)

he, she, you (formal)

we

they, you (plural)

like
play
work
need
I

favorite pastime
favorite season
favorite color
my

the net, the pole, the bat, the court, the glove, the ball, the basketball

never	at times	in the a.m.	in the p.m.	often	every day	always

GARDEN: Chapter Summary

A different flower or plant is used to represent the different verbs and verbal structures in the chapter. This particular chapter in the textbook contained only verbal ideas. One flower or plant should be used per concept.

Following the line of thinking behind visualization, the students should be given a visual wrap-up or recap sheet at the end of each unit before the unit test. Some variety in the visual wrap-ups should be presented.

HOW TO USE THE VISUAL DIAGRAM

1. Elicit from the students the first, second, and third person singular, then the plurals of each verb. The forms should be written in order in the flower. When the correct forms have been elicited, the drill is complete.

2. For such concepts as "have to" and "going to," it would be a good idea to elicit more than the verb forms. Try some easy sentences such as: I have to work. Do you have to go? He is going to work. We are not going to learn.

3. The first person should always be in the same place on each flower. For Spanish it is necessary for students to see how the nosotros form is different from the other stem-changing verb forms, thus this form must be highlighted in some way—by being in the same place on an extended petal, or by being shaded in, or written in with a different color.

1-114

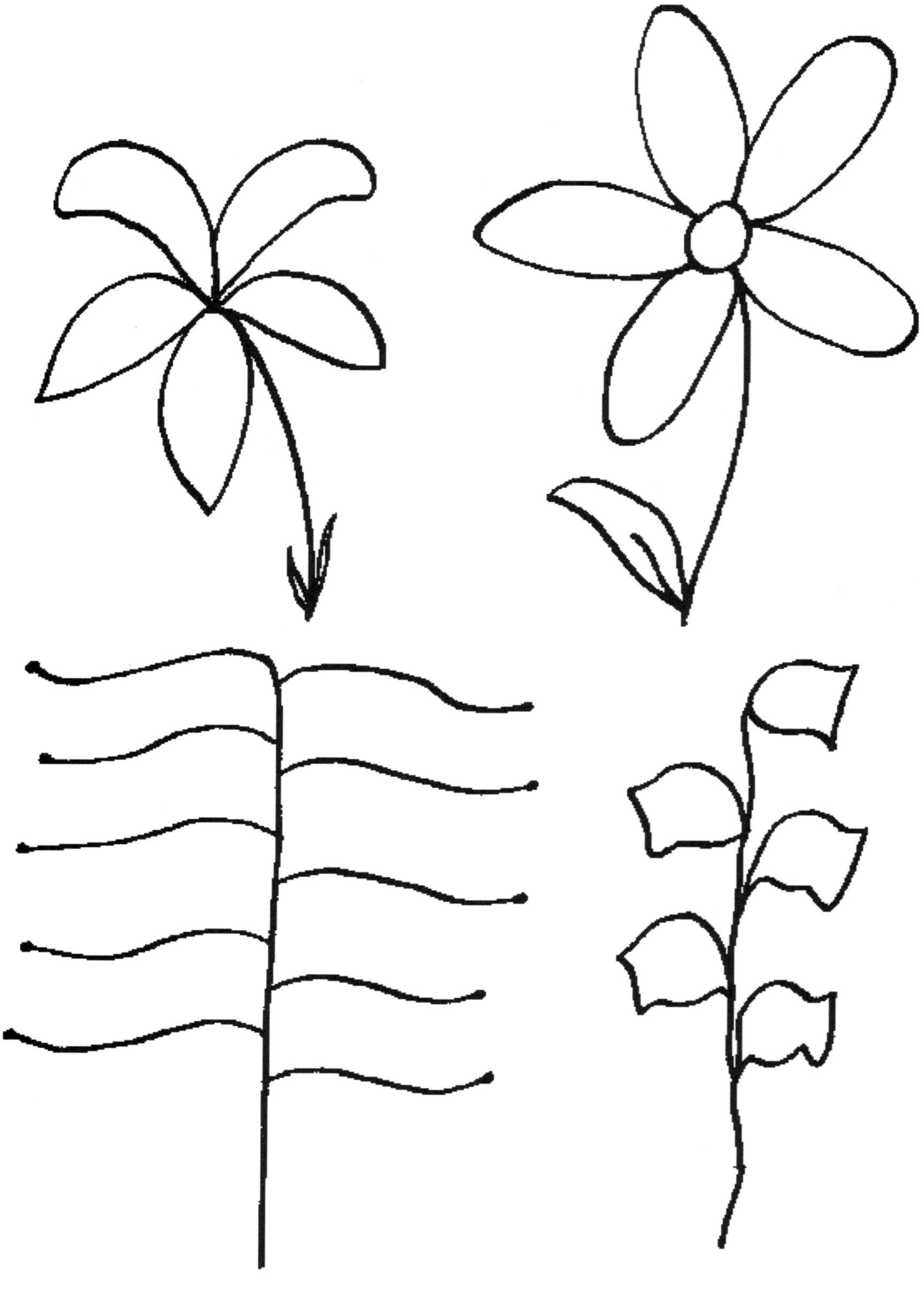

1-115

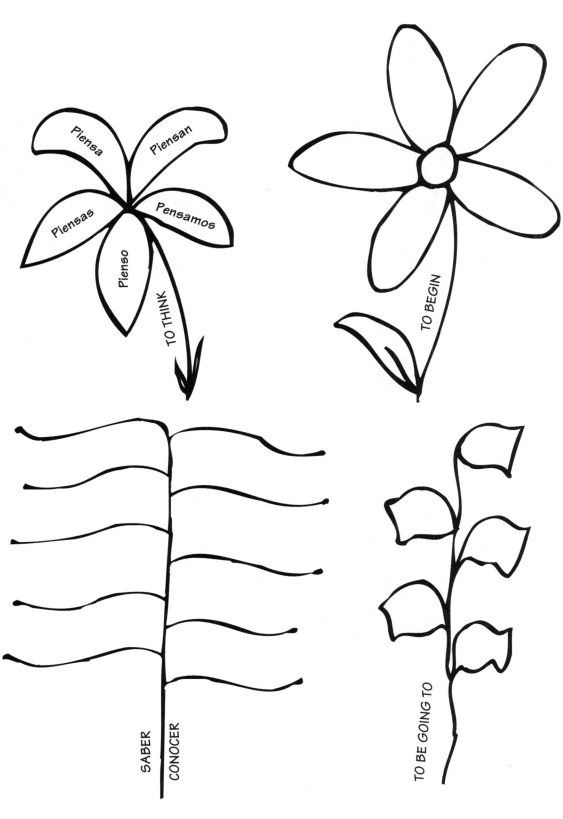

215

1-116

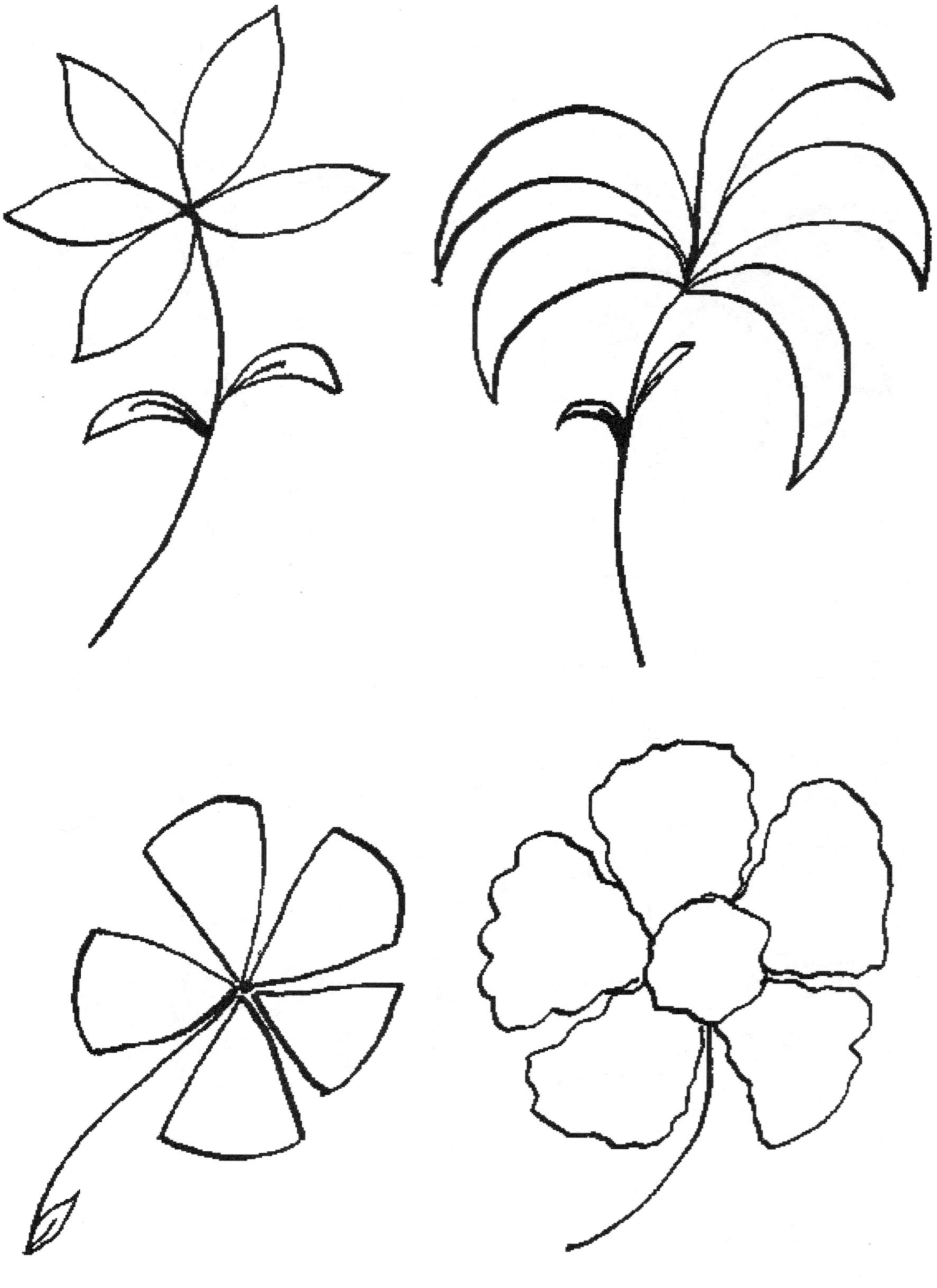

1-117

TO BE ABLE TO

(CAN)

TO HAVE TO

TO LEAVE

TO GO OUT

TO TELL

TO SAY

CALENDAR: Chapter Summary

A copy of any calendar month, preferably the actual month in which this exercise is being performed, may be used to summarize the vocabulary and grammar used in each unit. The calendar should contain the days of the week in the target language. Each day of the calendar will represent one word, one expression, or one grammatical concept.

HOW TO USE THE VISUAL DIAGRAM

1. Students should label the month in the target language.

2. To personalize the calendar, ask who has a birthday or special day during the month. In the target language, the students write on their calendar who has a birthday on which day. This may then be done with the various holidays celebrated that month.

3. After all preliminary discussions have ended, instruct the students in the target language to find the first day. On that day, students are to write the word, expression, or verbal form chosen by you.

4. Proceed until all the days contain an item from the chapter.

5. Reverting to the first day, ask the class what they have written for May 1, or November, or February—whatever month you use. After instructing the students to correct their own papers, continue until the last day of the month.

6. Students can isolate what they know and don't know.

7. To recapitulate the correct answers, draw the students back to May 1, repeat the correct answer, then await the choral repetition of the correct answer from the class.

el mes: _____

lunes	martes	miércoles	jueves	viernes	sábado	domingo

1-119

le mois: _____

lundi	mardi	mercredi	jeudi	vendredi	samedi	dimanche

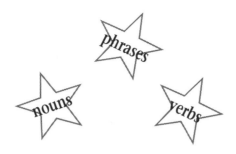

Part Two

VOCABULARY

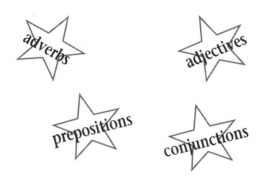

VOCABULARY AND SPELLING GRID

PURPOSE: To review basic vocabulary with reinforcement of correct spelling

INTRODUCTION: As students learn the basic vocabulary, you may want to proceed by syllables in reinforcing the spelling just prior to testing the words that students have already mastered orally. The following activity should follow oral mastery.

PROCEDURE

1. Working in the DIAS DE LA SEMANA column, ask the students the word for MONDAY. When the correct word, LUNES, is given, students should write the word by syllables, LU on line 1, NES on line 2. You may need to model the syllables for the students.

2. Ask for the word TUESDAY. When the word MARTES is volunteered, students should write MAR on line 3, TES on line 4.

3. Proceed until all the days of the week have been reviewed. Then ask students to exchange papers.

4. Show the overhead with answers. Each student should match the paper against the overhead, line by line. Where there is an error, the line should be crossed out. At the end, papers should be returned to their owners.

5. The owner rewrites the correct syllable according to the correct answer on the overhead.

6. Proceed with the next topic. In this case it is LAS MATERIAS.

7. The native language is already written to the side. Ask students to volunteer the word for LUNCH. When ALMUERZO is given, repeat it by syllables so that the students can fill in the lines.

8. Proceed to the end of the topic and correct as before.

9. Another sheet could be made up to include LOS NUMEROS, or any other topic that may be appropriate. Months of the year or classroom objects might be conducive to this type of drill.

10. Space is allowed at the bottom of the page for rewrites of corrections.

Comment: This kind of activity gives students the opportunity to hone in on several sound combinations, such as UE, EI, or IE, as well as the more simple vowel sounds.

2-1

DIAS DE LA SEMANA		LAS MATERIAS	
1.	**LUNCH**	1.	
2.		2.	
3.		3.	
4.	**PHYSICS**	4.	
5.		5.	
6.		6.	
7.	**SCIENCE**	7.	
8.		8.	
9.		9.	
10.		10.	
11.	**HISTORY**	11.	
12.		12.	
13.		13.	
14.		14.	
15.	**ART**	15.	
16.		16.	
17.			
18.			
19.			

SYLLABLE REWRITES:

DIAS DE LA SEMANA		LAS MATERIAS	
1. LU	LUNCH	1. AL	
2. NES		2. MUER	
3. MAR		3. ZO	
4. TES	PHYSICS	4. FI	
5. MI		5. SI	
6. ER		6. CA	
7. CO	SCIENCE	7. CI	
8. LES		8. EN	
9. JUE		9. CI	
10. VES		10. A	
11. VI	HISTORY	11. HI	
12. ER		12. STO	
13. NES		13. RI	
14. SA		14. A	
15. BA	ART	15. AR	
16. DO		16. TE	
17. DO			
18. MIN			
19. GO			

SYLLABLE REWRITES:

VOCAB TAB SOLITAIRE

PURPOSE: To teach the most important vocabulary words of a given chapter or section

PREPARATION: Cut strips of paper into small squares or rectangles approximately 2″ × 2″, enough to be bent in half yet big enough to be written on both halves. Each student should receive one square per important vocabulary word. If there are 10 salient words, then the student should be given 10 squares. This is a revision of the classic flash card concept.

PROCEDURE

1. The student bends the paper in half, forming a little tent.

2. On one side, as you pronounce the target word correctly, the student writes the target language word as it is written in the text, on the board, on a vocabulary sheet, or any other source of accurate spelling. On the other side, the student writes the native language.

3. After the students have filled out all the vocab tabs, they line them up, like tents, on their own desks.

4. Pronounce each word, having students repeat each word after you.

5. As in the game of solitaire, students now spend time, in silence, in front of the target language side of the folded papers. They try to guess the native language meaning of each word. A successful guess means that the vocab tabs are turned around so that the native language is facing the students. If they miss, they must return to those words at the end of the run. Students should successfully guess the meaning of all the words before proceeding to the next step.

6. Now that the recognition step has been successfully tested, it is time for the recall step. Now facing the native language, students should guess the target language words. At the end of the round, all students should be facing the target words. This indicates 100 percent success. If students make a mistake, or forget the correct response, they should look at the correct word, but leave the vocab tab with the native language in front. At the end of the run, students should return to their mistaken vocab tabs and guess, once again, until they achieve 100 percent mastery.

7. Pass the stapler or a paper clip to each student so that they can protect their "vocab pack." Because students may lose their packs, you may want to collect them, with their names on the top vocab tab, then distribute them the next day.

8. On the following day(s), each student chooses five vocab tabs as a mini quiz for a partner.

9. Partner A sets out the five vocab tabs with the native language facing Partner B, and verifies that Partner B provides the correct answer. (This may be done with a third partner, if necessary.)

10. Partner B then sets out five tabs as indicated above.

11. Students can then take their five vocab tabs to those students who have already finished. This can be repeated many times over many days, especially as an initial warmup. Times will vary. Generally, there are slow and fast learners in the same class.

12. From solitaire to cooperative learning, students can now proceed with another set of vocabulary words.

ALTERNATIVE: This alternative would require more teacher preparation, but it would ensure target language accuracy. There seem to be more and more students in our classes with different varieties of dyslexia or learning disabilities. For these students, who are certainly capable of learning another language, you can do the following:

1. On a standard or legal size piece of paper, draw the tabs, but print clearly, with big letters, the target language word to be learned. This will allow the students to write in the native language meaning, thus allowing some participation in the learning process.

2. Copy the paper, to allow one sheet of all the words for each student.

3. Either use the paper cutter to cut the words, or bring scissors so that students can cut out their own tabs.

OUTER PERIPHERAL VOCABULARY LEARNING

EXPLANATION

In this mobile version of solitaire, students move from desk to desk, as the teacher directs. It uses the vocab tab idea of the previous activity. This can be used to review the words already learned, or to teach words for the first time. Ideally, there will be one word per student. There may even be two words per student.

PROCEDURE

1. Make up a number of vocab tabs (small flash cards folded in half, like tents, with the target language on one half, and the native language on the other half). Place vocab tabs on each desk around the periphery of the classroom, or you may choose to give a vocab tab to each student, to place on each desk. The number of students, desks, and vocab tabs are all variables in this exercise; however, the concept can be very effective, and is certainly worth a try.

   If this is a review, the tabs should show the native language to the students so that they will guess the target language; if it is used to teach new, unfamiliar vocabulary, the students should face the target language.

2. Direct students to stand behind a desk that has a vocab tab on it.

3. If this is a review, have students look at the native language word, silently guess the target language word, then check to verify correctness. The word should stay in the native language position.

   If this is a first-time learning situation, repeat each word, followed by student repetition. It is vital to maintain the integrity of proper pronunciation. This should be followed by the instruction to pick up each vocab tab, and note the native language meaning of each word.

4. Then instruct—in the target language—"to the left" (a clockwise formation), at which point, students move to the next desk and repeat the process. This is done until the students have returned to their starting desks.

5. If the words are new to the students, it may be advantageous to go around (the clock) a second time. If not a second time on that first day, then it should be repeated the next day of class.

6. Ask the students to gather the words on each desk, to bring them to the front, for you to pick a vocab tab at random. Then give the native language meaning, to which the students should chorally, or individually, respond with the desired target language. This will give you an idea of how well the vocabulary has been learned.

Students enjoy moving around. This exercise enables them not only to move around, but also to quantify the words they need to learn. An added crutch is that they may remember which word is on whose desk.

STAR REVIEW

PURPOSE: To review vocabulary prior to a quiz or test. The star formation allows students to isolate the vocabulary they still don't know.

PREPARATION: One copy of the star should be given to each student.

PROCEDURE

1. Ask the students to locate the number one on the star, next to which the students should write the target language word that corresponds to the native language word you have chosen. For example, to elicit the words <u>la casa</u> or <u>la maison</u>, say "house."

2. Proceed as above until all numbers on the star have a word next to them.

3. Students then exchange papers.

4. Students are to cross out the wrong answers as the corrections are given, either by the students or by you.

5. Students are then instructed to connect any two numbers next to each other that are correct.

6. A completely connected star indicates that a student knows all the vocabulary.

7. As students examine their stars, you may want to repeat with the students all the words tested.

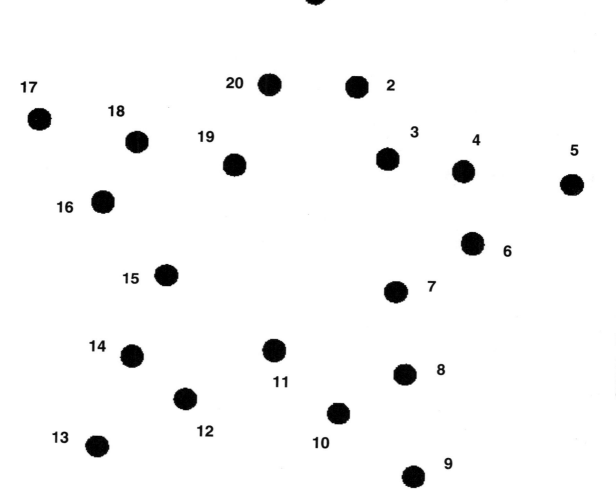

VOCABULARY BOOKLET

PURPOSE: To isolate the most difficult words of the chapter, or a section, with the intent of memorizing them by using the solitaire approach.

PREPARATION: Distribute cut-up paper strips from legal size paper to each student. Cut lengthwise. Each strip should be approximately two inches wide. One strip provides one drill booklet containing five native language and five target language words.

PROCEDURE

1. Instruct the students to hold the paper lengthwise, then to fold it in half three times.

2. Students should now unfold the paper to check that there are eight little boxes ready to be filled.

3. Students now bend the paper to form a book with the open, front flap facing to the right.

4. On the cover of the minibook (look at Back 8A on diagram) students are to write the native language word you give them, for example, "sick."

5. On the flip side (8B on diagram), students are instructed to write the target language, for example, malade or enfermo.

6. Facing the students is the third box (7A) on which another native language word should be written.

7. On box 4 (6B), behind box 3, the target language should be written.

8. The above procedure should be followed until 10 boxes have been completed. The tenth box is 1B, the back of the last item. It will represent a target language word.

9. As you repeat each target language word, the students should also repeat the word.

10. Having heard the correct pronunciation, students now should "work the book." As in solitaire, they should look at the native language word, then guess the target language word, or look at the target language word for the purpose of memorizing the meaning.

11. When students run through the whole book they should repeat this a second time.

12. A second book, preferably a colored one, could be made with five new words.

13. On the same day, or the following day, students should test a partner by using the book. The native language word is given to elicit the new target word.

14. Students can keep their booklets, or you can collect them after they have written their names on the book covers.

Comment: This may appear to be too time-consuming a task for only a small amount of words. However, once students have learned how to make the first booklet, the task becomes easier. This tool does allow you to highlight the most difficult words. It is not recommended for every word in every chapter.

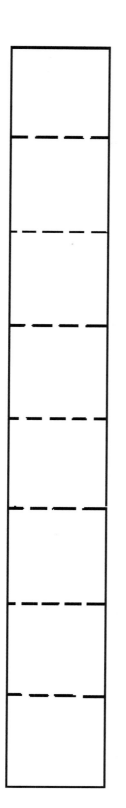

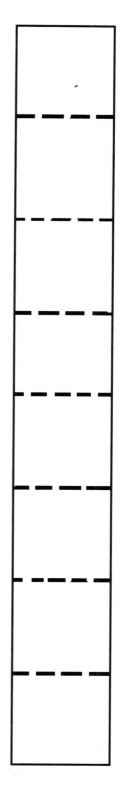

2-5

Front:

8b la casa	7a dining room	6b el comedor	5a bathroom	4b el baño	3a the garden	2b el jardín	1a the living room

Back:

house 8a							la sala 1b

KEY to VOCABULARY BOOKLET DIAGRAM:

- - - - - - = fold

————— | ————— = cut

a = native language

b = target language

PASS THE WORD ALONG

PURPOSE: To visually teach the meaning of vocabulary as conceived by the students in an atmosphere of silent learning

PREPARATION: Distribute small pieces of paper, squares large enough for students to be able to design their own interpretation of the meaning. Students may be given any number of pieces of paper. Each piece represents a single word or image.

PROCEDURE

1. From the text or vocabulary list, assign one word to each student for that student to design on the square. If the word is "sick" the student should design his or her interpretation of that word or idea.

2. Students must label their picture(s) with the target language word.

3. Ask the students to surround your desk.

4. Look at each word and repeat it, followed by student repetition of each word to ensure proper pronunciation.

5. Students are instructed to silently make a word-picture association in their minds.

6. In the target language, call "to the left" (clockwise), at which time the students silently pass their artwork to the next person.

7. Students should now commit to memory the picture and the word on the square they have just received; they should feel free to ask "What is this?"

8. Now call "to the left" again—until every word has been passed around once.

9. Announce that the words will go around one more time, but at a faster pace.

10. The next day in class, this should be repeated, even though some students will be absent and those absent on the previous day will have returned. Flexibility is always *de rigueur*.

Comment: "Outer Peripheral Vocabulary Learning" and "Pass the Word Along" drills attempt to use the classroom purposefully in the effective learning of vocabulary. The added bonus is student participation in designing the concept—words as keys to a specific reality or idea. For the teacher, an added bonus is the laughter—the audible manifestation of enjoyment at learning words.

LOST IN THE FOREST

PREPARATION: Draw a lost-in-the forest scene on the board, similar to the illustration, or use the transparency master. Plot a native language word at each of the twelve "milestones."

PROCEDURE

1. Place twelve native language words, one per stone, on the overhead, or copied version at the board.

2. Ask the students to listen to, and learn from one another, then explain that the goal is to guess each word correctly so that someone may rescue the group by reaching the safety station.

3. In a homogeneously grouped class, you may want to begin with the first student in class. In a mixed-level class, ask for volunteers. Avoid choosing the strongest student, who will be able to guess every word correctly the first time. This would prevent the benefit of focused attention and drill on all the words. Also avoid choosing the weakest student whose self-image is at stake.

4. Ask the first student the target language word for the first word on the board. If the student misses, the student's initials can be written before the first word. If the student correctly says the word, he or she will advance to the second word, and so forth until he or she misses. The student's initials are placed at the last correct vocabulary word.

5. If the first student has not reached the safety station at the top of the mountain ("home"), the second student starts behind number one. Ask the same first word. The student will either have his or her initials left at the scene, or advance.

6. Dramatize the rescue scene. For example, student one is the first pioneer to scout out the territory. Those students who have all faltered at one word can sit together and really get to know each other. The snakes, bears and other forest animals are meant to dramatize the danger of the rescue situation.

7. Once a student has guessed the meaning of every word, thus reaching the safety station at the end, you should also dramatize the victory.

2-7

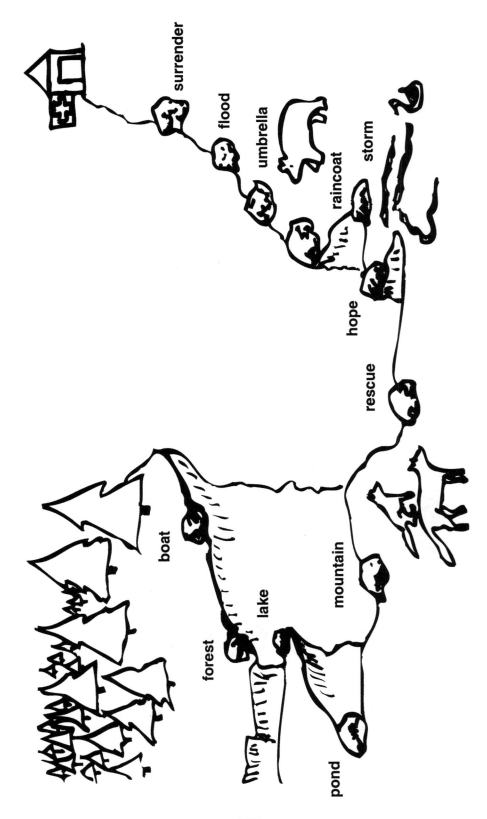

surrender
flood
umbrella
raincoat
storm
hope
rescue
boat
lake
forest
mountain
pond

©1995 by The Center for Applied Research in Education

238

GRAPHIC VOCABULARY

PURPOSE: To establish the meaning of new vocabulary words by having all students design their conception of the words

PREPARATION: Hand out to each student a copy of the target language vocabulary to be learned, and mastered. (Use reproducible following this activity.)

PROCEDURE

1. Students are directed first to repeat the words after you pronounce them, then to draw their conception of the word based on the definition given in the text or from the vocabulary sheet. This will take some time.

2. Students will finish at different times. You will see who is a sketch drawer and who is detail oriented. Those who finish first should begin to memorize the picture with the word.

3. Once all students have finished, direct them to write their names on their papers, to exchange their artwork with another student, then to memorize the word-picture association from the new paper.

4. Students are then directed to exchange papers with another person before they return them to the original owners.

5. This may be done as many times as you deem necessary.

6. For a homework assignment, students could write the new word two more times in the box.

Comments: This exercise does not need to be limited to fifteen words, nor does it limit itself to concrete vocabulary, although it is most amenable to it. Concepts such as "liberty" or "pride" could be reduced to a graphic image.

The exercise has proven enjoyable to students and to teachers largely because of the smiles and laughter generated from the students' artwork. Everyone is impressed by the idea that we all see things differently. The many different pictures sketched to represent one vocabulary word function as hooks to assist the students in learning the meanings.

el libro	el bolígrafo	la goma	el cuaderno	el pupitre
el escritorio	la silla	el rincón	el papel	la maestra
la escuela	el reloj	el estante	el horario	el alumno

ARTIST-IN-RESIDENCE VOCABULARY

PURPOSE: To teach the meaning of vocabulary visually, as conceived by a master artist—either a student or you.

PREPARATION: Have a student volunteer design the image of each targeted vocabulary word on a sheet of paper to be photocopied for all students, or you may choose to do it. Reuse the visual diagram from "Graphic Vocabulary." A line is drawn at the top so that the students can find the word in their vocabulary list, then write it a couple of times.

PROCEDURE

1. Hand out a predrawn xeroxed sheet of paper to each student. On it are the designs that the student artist, or teacher, has made of the pertinent vocabulary.

2. Ask the students to find the words in their vocabulary list, then to write the words one or two times in the box.

3. After you pronounce each word, the students should repeat them to ensure proper pronunciation.

4. If there are enough scissors in class, the students can cut the vocabulary words to separate them, or they can rip them along the lines after folding them to create a crease.

5. The students should place these new artist-designed vocabulary cards on their desks and begin to memorize the meanings by attaching the image to the word.

6. Students can then work with a partner.

7. Partner work can take the following forms:

   a. Partner 1 lays all but three cards on the desk. Partner 2 must guess, in the target language, which three are missing. The roles should now be reversed.

   b. Partner 1 picks five words, as in a mini quiz. By bending back the word, or by covering up the word, partner 1 shows only the image for which partner 2 should guess the meaning. Roles can now be reversed.

8. Partner 1 can hold five cards in his or her hand without showing the hand to partner 2. Partner 2 has five chances to guess which five they are. This is similar to a pick-5 lotto. The number can be reduced to three, as in a pick 3-lotto, if that number is more manageable. The roles can then be reversed.

POSTER ART

PURPOSE: To teach vocabulary by categories or according to themes

INTRODUCTION: Many catalogues offer thematic vocabulary to be taught in many visual ways, but at great cost. The catalogues do serve as a good source of inspiration for topics. There is, however, a special personal investment of student talent and interest when the students make their own posters, as big and as colorfully as they want. Student presentations of the vocabulary will be varied.

SUGGESTIONS

1. You may have to provide colored poster board and necessary drawing instruments unless students can provide their own.

2. Cutouts from magazines and newspapers can be used for less artistic students.

3. Students should be given the target language and native language translation of each word; however, only the target language should appear on the poster. The word should be printed either on or close to the picture in large, dark print.

4. Before all work is posted, first encourage the students to edit their work for accuracy, then you conduct the last review.

5. Suggested list of possible topics:

weather	seasons	colors (done as a rainbow)
animals	occupations	fruit
beverages	vegetables	meat
emotions	body parts	transportation

THEMES:

shopping	haunted house	religious celebrations
birthday	holidays	picnics
phrases		

Use any other suggestions provided by the many commercial conversation books that present vocabulary by themes.

6. Posters may teach many vocabulary words or an individual idea, such as "I love you."

PUZZLE

PURPOSE: To present or drill concrete thematic vocabulary

INTRODUCTION: Where vocabulary is presented by text as a scene, for example, a carnival, a farm, or a city, the scene can be xeroxed (using the reproducible) enlarged, then cut into puzzle pieces around the essential vocabulary. Another suggestion would be to have the students draw the scene on a large piece of light-colored construction paper. The paper could then be cut into significant pieces. If duplication is done, several copies could be preserved to show the finished version of the puzzle, or as a reference.

PROCEDURE

1. Each student may be assigned a word as part of the thematic unit. A large paper could be passed from student to student on which each would sketch his or her target word. One student might be willing to take the completed paper overnight and color it.

2. Cut the pieces then place into a labeled envelope, large or small, according to the size of the puzzle.

3. Empty the pieces onto a flat surface from which students will pick a piece for which they know the target word. As the piece is placed on a flat surface (perhaps your desk), the student must pronounce the word. This occurs until every new word has become integrated into the scene. It will focus everyone's attention on the vocabulary.

4. This activity has potential for competitive races, if desired. Two teams can be given the envelope of pictures. A member from each team withdraws one picture, names it, then integrates it with the other puzzle pieces. The first team to name all pieces successfully wins.

5. Another possibility for an initial presentation of vocabulary is to open an envelope with already cut-up pieces, each representing a word from the list. You might prefer that the students not see the initial picture, but rather, be led to discover the scope of the scene by themselves.

6. As each student is given a piece to identify from the vocabulary list, the individual student takes responsibility for teaching the new word to the group, by saying the word he or she just looked up, then placing it on a flat surface to be integrated with other pieces. This can be done only if the students have a good basis of the target language sound system.

GRAFFITI WALL

PURPOSE: To practice the target vocabulary at the board

PROCEDURE

1. Assign to each student a word from the target list, which the student will then formulate into a sentence—a short sentence, if there are a lot of students. If there are not enough words for each student to have one, words may be duplicated. It is interesting to see the different ways words can be put into sentences.

2. Circulate to the desks of students who have difficulty composing sentences.

STUDENT-GENERATED BORDERS

3. As each student finishes a sentence at the board, he or she should surround it with a border to offset the sentence. Give ideas of borders: moon, sun, star, simple animal, baseball.

4. Students should underline the target word.

5. To add variety, use colored chalk.

6. As some of the slower students finish their sentences at the board, you may begin at one end of the board. You stand next to the designs with their featured sentences, and correct the blatant errors as each artist reads his or her sentence. You may want to point out errors of plurals, genders, and spelling to put the finishing touches on students' work.

7. Where students create provocative sentences, you may wish to ask questions, in the target language, about the information. Engaging interest in the word, which creates an idea, is important to stress and to pursue. Words are keys to ideas. Allow students to enjoy the process of communicating in a foreign language within this academic setting of vocabulary drilling.

TEACHER-GENERATED BORDERS

8. An alternative, which serves the same purpose but which adds variety, is the teacher-generated border system whereby the teacher creates a puzzle piece effect on the board, with colored chalk, or designs desired borders. You may also use the transparency master.

9. Into each design students will write their sentences with the new words. Students may want to initial their sentences.

2-10

246

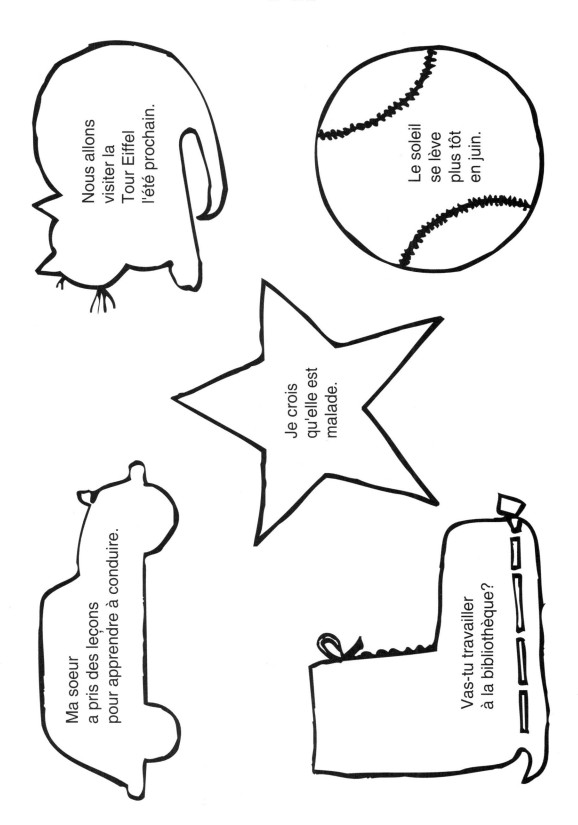

Nous allons visiter la Tour Eiffel l'été prochain.

Le soleil se lève plus tôt en juin.

Je crois qu'elle est malade.

Ma soeur a pris des leçons pour apprendre à conduire.

Vas-tu travailler à la bibliothèque?

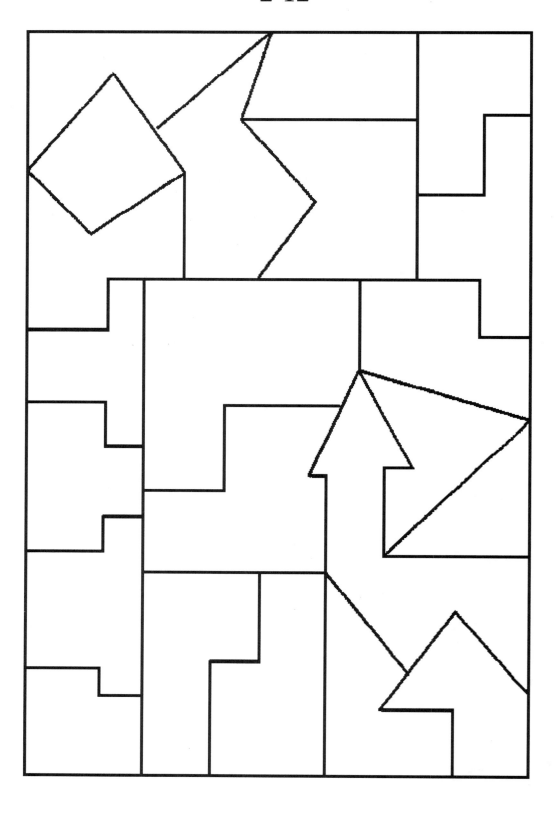

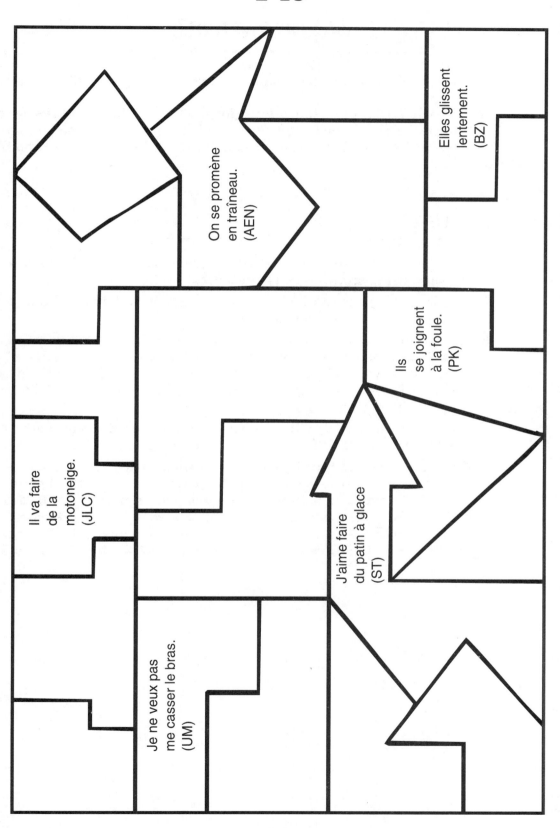

Elles glissent lentement. (BZ)

On se promène en traîneau. (AEN)

Ils se joignent à la foule. (PK)

Il va faire de la motoneige. (JLC)

J'aime faire du patin à glace (ST)

Je ne veux pas me casser le bras. (UM)

BINGO DRILL

PURPOSE: To reinforce the meaning of vocabulary by engaging attention

INTRODUCTION: Prior to testing a long list of vocabulary words, such as the end of a chapter or of a section, students should make a standard bingo board, which can be renamed PADRE for Spanish classes, PARIS in French classes, and SPIEL in German classes.

PROCEDURE

1. Students choose twenty-five target language words from their list by placing one word per space, with no spare spaces.

2. Students are encouraged to keep lists handy for reference if they forget the meaning of the words they have chosen.

3. Call out in the native language the translation for each word. If you call "the house," the students must have "la casa," "la maison," or "Das Haus" on their boards. If they chose the word, they are to place one diagonal mark through the box. (If students cross out the whole word completely, it will be impossible to verify the selected words.)

4. When a student has any five vertical, horizontal, or diagonal spaces, he or she should call "PADRE," "PARIS," or "SPIEL" to signify a win.

5. Verify the student's board, and you may want to give a prize, such as a piece of candy. Students will clamor to continue until second or third place has been revealed. To maintain interest in reinforcing meaning, it might be advisable to continue the drill. Students have the motivation to refer to the meaning from their vocabulary lists. Even slower students can win at this. An added bonus for students is the extra written reinforcement of writing the target language words.

2-14

P	A	D	R	E

P	A	R	I	S

S	P	I	E	L

TIC-TAC-TOE DRILL

PURPOSE: To reinforce the meaning of words by engaging attention

INTRODUCTION: Prior to testing a short group of words, students should make a standard tic-tac-toe board, or you can copy the reproducible.

PROCEDURE

1. Students choose nine target language words from their vocabulary list and place one word per space, with no spare space. Students are encouraged to keep lists handy for reference if they should forget the meaning of their chosen words.

2. Explain that the goal is to get all nine correct answers. Each answer should be marked with one diagonal mark through the box so that it will be possible for you to verify the winner's answers.

3. Call out the word in the native language, the translation for each vocabulary word, as in the previous "Bingo Drill."

4. When students have all nine words, they should call out the foreign language equivalent of "I have it" or "I won."

5. Verify the winner's board, and you may want to award a prize.

6. Since students will want to continue for second and third place, it is advisable to continue so that more students will have an opportunity to win—and while motivation runs high—to learn or reinforce meaning. Where interest runs high, so will attentiveness to the words.

Note that this drill gives students an extra opportunity to write the target language words.

BASEBALL DRILL

PURPOSE: To drill a large vocabulary list in each chapter just prior to a test or exam

PROCEDURE

1. The class is divided into Team A and Team B (see the reproducible).

2. A student from each team comes to the center seat, starting in seat 2.

3. Ask student A for the target language definition of a word given in the native language. If student A correctly says the word, that student moves to seat 1 of Team A. An incorrect answer requires that the student remain in seat 2.

4. Student B is then asked a word, and moves to seat 1 if the answer is correct.

5. Returning to student A, give another word to define in the target language. If successful, the student moves from seat 1 back to the Team A lineup. The student has earned a homerun, and a replacement from Team A is now chosen to begin at seat 2.

6. The student from Team B is given an opportunity to guess a word correctly in order to win a run and return to the lineup. Again, if a mistake is made, the student remains in the seat.

7. The drill may proceed until one team has used up all its players, thus scoring the most homeruns. The other team may be far behind, and not all students will have had the opportunity to drill words. To rectify this, the first attempt may be considered one inning, thus the drill can continue, perhaps until the bell rings.

8. You may choose to make a list of the words that students missed. Also, if a student from one team does not guess the target language word, the word may be recycled to the second team.

9. At the end of the drill, redrill the words most often missed. Student attention has been awakened, and they will probably be more ready to learn these words.

Caution: Show sensitivity toward the students of lesser ability by giving them easier words to recall while "at bat."

2-19

> [!NOTE]
> TEAM A

> [!NOTE]
> TEAM A

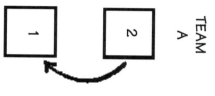

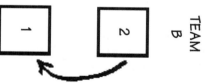

> [!NOTE]
> TEAM B

> [!NOTE]
> TEAM B

TRACING

PURPOSE: To establish visual meaning with the target vocabulary words

INTRODUCTION: Students may be used to memorizing a list of vocabulary words from target language to native language; however, to facilitate learning, and to provide greater retention of the vocabulary by providing visual hooks, this technique is suited for the initial presentation of the vocabulary.

Many textbooks have useful illustrations of vocabulary taught as part of a theme (a farm, a department store, etc.), or even as relatively disparate items. These illustrations are usually quite easily traceable.

PROCEDURE

1. Provide a piece of tracing paper to each student. The Mathematics Department generally has this type of paper, which is useful in tracing diagrams, as well as in tracing vocabulary words.

2. Have the students trace the pertinent objects, then label with the target language word on, inside, along the periphery, or as close to the object as possible. The students need a visual association with a single word. A homework assignment could be the rewriting of each new word two more times.

3. Once the meaning of the word has been established, pronounce the words with the students, then ask target language questions about the various words, for example, in a department store that features the words "bathrobe," or "slippers," students could be asked if they use these items. When students say "no," additional questions should be asked, such as, "What do you use instead of slippers?" or "Why don't you use slippers?" In this manner, other vocabulary is drawn into the discussion, such as "socks" or "barefoot." There is a sense of wholeness, and a sense of personal appropriation, or of claiming ownership, as the vocabulary becomes personalized and part of a discussion. The words are no longer relegated to a formal list. Once again, the idea of words as keys to ideas is reinforced. An added bonus is the opportunity for comical answers.

PICTURE BOOK

PURPOSE: To capitalize on an opportunity to use the functional-notional goal of asking and answering how the vacation was—of using vocabulary in a conversational setting the day after a vacation.

PROCEDURE

1. Hand out to each student a piece of blank paper, preferably a rectangular piece, which students should fold, first in half lengthwise, then twice the other way, so that they have six boxes into which they will draw small cartoons and dialogues.

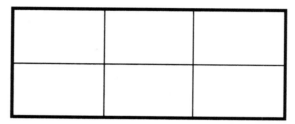

2. Holding the paper lengthwise, instruct students that they should fill in each of the six boxes with two simple cartoon heads or figures, starting with the first question, in the target language, "How was your vacation?" or "What did you do during the vacation?" In the same first box, the respondent should answer the question.

3. Students are to proceed with the same dialogue couple in each box until all six have been filled. You may wish to provide suggestions such as, "What movies did you watch?" "How did you get there?" "Did you like it?"

4. Once the boxes have been completed, students may get together in groups of two to take turns reading aloud the cartoons that each one has made, or they may just exchange papers with a neighbor to read silently. If the class is small, or large enough to divide into two groups, students may prefer sitting in one or two circles while papers are passed around in a clockwise direction. Silent reading takes place, usually interspersed with laughter at the drawings.

5. In classes where all students do their homework, teachers might choose to use this as a homework assignment the first night after the vacation. This way, students who are unable to draw may opt to cut out the heads of people in catalogues, newspapers, or magazines—if they can obtain enough of the same person to carry on a six-box dialogue. Students might also have at home a whole array of stickers, perhaps of smiling faces, or of clowns, or of stamps that could be used in place of drawing. This avoids any possible mockery of student drawings.

6. If you use this as homework, students should still be exposed to one another's work, thus, papers should be exchanged between students.

PRONUNCIATION DRILLS

INTRODUCTION: Students may be able to recall words, in oral or written form. Ideally, the students should be able to pronounce the vocabulary or the phrases with native pronunciation and fluency. To attain this, effective strategies are needed.

MATERIALS: A cassette player with native language tapes (a usual accompaniment to many textbooks), and written copy of the auditory tapes

PROCEDURE

1. As students look at the written text, establish meaning, line by line, or phrase by phrase.
2. Play the auditory tape while students are engaged in active listening.
3. Play the tape again while the whole class reads together by lip-synching.
4. Play the tape again while the whole class, in unison, whispers the text while listening to the pronunciation and speed of the tape.
5. Play the tape again while the whole class, in unison, drones through the text. This time, the students are familiar with the breaks in the text, so they should be able to begin and end the phrases at the appropriate time.
6. If students have a short attention span, one of the steps above, preferably Step 5, could be eliminated.
7. Finally, without the tapes, ask individual students to read the text at the same speed and with the same pronunciation they heard on the tapes. At this point they will have had enough native modeling.

READING COMPREHENSION GUIDE

PURPOSE: To help poor readers grasp the focus of the reading by providing some initial introductions in response to basic questions

PREPARATION: Write on the board, in the target language, the target questions:

WHO   WHAT   WHEN   WHERE   HOW   WHY

PROCEDURE

1. Before the reading begins, list the answer to the basic questions, such as, <u>who</u>, <u>when</u> and <u>where</u> of either the beginning of the story or of the whole tale.

2. If there are poor readers in the class, you may want to provide more information as to <u>what</u> is going to happen.

3. Now the students can focus on the <u>what</u>, <u>how</u>, and especially, the <u>why</u> of the story.

4. After the story has been read, elicit from the students the answers to the other questions. The answers will then be written on the board, or the overhead, if you are using one. From this, you may begin to ask comprehension questions, such as, "Can you describe Mr. X?" or "Where did Mr. X go after the party?"

Comment: While readers are supposed to be comprehending <u>what</u> is happening and <u>why</u> it is happening, they are often still bogged down on the <u>who</u> and the <u>where</u>.

VOCABULARY AND GRAMMAR IN VERSE

PURPOSE: To put the text contents into rhyming couplets to tell a story or to create an image.

Those games and other delightful change-of-pace activities that purport to activate interest and to energize learning efforts on the part of language learning students become more vital as the school year progresses, especially as students and teachers face the winter doldrums. Conferences that offer lectures or seminars on entertaining ideas in FL teaching seem to draw greater numbers than do the more didactic ones. Teachers constantly seek ways in which to disguise rigorous learning by providing the diversion that students seek. (It would be music to our ears to hear students comment that they had enjoyed the learning process in our classrooms.)

Two related exercises grew out of the need for diversion within the context of solidifying learning—exercises that used the text content as the source of learning.

Reading through Chapter 15 ("Ski Au Québec") of *Nos Amis*, (Harcourt Brace Jovanovich), I was struck by the numbers of rhyming words in the reading material, and the next day's typical class assignment was changed. My ninth-graders were asked to make rhyming couplets from the text with the goal of retelling the story. After finding five sets of rhyming couplets, students wrote them on the board, reading them aloud. Corrections were made at the time, and repeated ideas were erased. Gradually, we could assign numbers to the rhyming couplets in order to organize the material into a chronologically accurate poem.

In a more advanced class, groups of students proceeded from rhyming couplets to the production of their own chronologically accurate poems. Each group submitted a poem, which was then typed, xeroxed, and distributed for class reading the next day.

My ninth-grade Spanish class had a different experience with the text; Chapter 21 ("Un Domingo en la Playa") of *Nuestros Amigos* (Harcourt Brace Jovanovich) provided text without a chronology of events. Because the vocabulary presentation was geared to the creation of an image, that of a day at the beach in Puerto Rico, the class was grouped into cells of four students. Their assignment was to create five sets of rhyming couplets to be grouped into a poem format representing the theme. A cell leader was chosen to edit and to record the final effort.

With the cell group actively engaged, their teacher was released to assist students in balancing sentences, correcting grammar, or rephrasing ideas according to the level of their grammatical knowledge. This activity lends itself to teaching a new, short, structural concept to a group, which might be able to absorb and manipulate it more easily than if it were presented to a whole class. It would also provide a challenge to those students whose interest is piqued by new linguistic avenues.

An example of rephrasing "Yo me siento y miro. . ." might be "Me siento para mirar. . ." The "para" plus infinitive concept could easily be taught at a time when the students were ready to receive such instruction. It would then be your option as to whether the whole class could be taught this concept the next day at the time of oral readings of the class poems.

Reproducing for each student all the poems created is a necessary step. Again, it would be your option as to whether a spirit of competition should reign by the awarding of prizes to the best poem. Where there are several classes of the same subject, it is interesting to see how many different versions of the poem can be generated by the different classes. Each class can judge the poems of the others. Another step could be the illustration of such poems by the artistically inclined students. Integrating the creations into a departmental or school foreign language newspaper is another possibility.

What had transpired, and what had been accomplished both affectively and academically during the creation of such rhyming couplets?

Affectively, students experienced joy at their individual contribution and cooperative accomplishment—the clever reworking of vocabulary and grammar into comprehensible and more appealing forms than that of the text. Since knowledge of the text was an essential preliminary step, the students had an incentive to do the actual reading and rereading of it. In addition to the feeling of having superseded the quality of the text's presentation, was the sense of deep knowledge of the grammar, vocabulary, and expressions used in the chapter—a depth of knowledge many students had never before plumbed. That sense of mastery engendered a tremendous amount of satisfaction. Rhyming had become a game, a musical diversion.

From an academic standpoint, the collaboration among students was constructive for them and delightful for the teacher to behold. Searching for that melodic rhyme caused the students to interact enthusiastically with one another. Testing out the sound quality, students were constantly engaged in repeating the words aloud and to themselves. Others in the group took charge of manipulating words for meaning by verifying the definitions and genders. One example of this comes to mind as students tried to fit:

Veo a la chica lindísima

este día hermosísima. (error)

A perceptive student recognized that día was masculine, thus requiring a change in hermosísima. An alternative structure had to be manipulated to rhyme with the original statement. Small challenges, small goals, all of this became a word game.

Notes taken on this activity recall such questions as, "What's an 'orilla'?" and statements such as, "No we can't use this because it needs 'estar'," and queries such as, "What do we do with these reflexive verbs?" This last query enabled the teacher to demonstrate the manipulation of reflexive structures such as the changing of podemos broncearnos to nos podemos broncear.

Witnessing the interaction of students with the material as well as with each other—with the culmination of a linguistic group effort—proved more valuable than the original activity still in the teacher's planbook. Besides the affective and academic fulfillment, we were able to integrate the individual performance objectives and goals for our language classes in terms of oral, auditory, and written work.

SAMPLES: FRENCH CLASSES

Cell Group A

C'est la saison préférée
de Denise et Louise Goulet.
C'est la saison de ski,
et tous les samedis,
sauf quand il fait trop mauvais,
leur père les emmène.
Après leur arrivée,
elles achètent leurs billets,
et vont au chalet
pour se préparer.
Elles ont leurs propres skis, heureusement,
car il faut faire la queue longtemps
pour l'équipement.
En haut de la montagne elles sont allées,
mais Denise est tombée.
Louise l'a aidée à se relever.
Denise est descendue au chalet
pour se reposer.
Jocelyne a trouvé
que Denise devrait aller
à l'infirmerie.
Raymond est allé
chercher Paul, un de ses amis.
Elle a marché
et a appris
que la jambe n'est pas cassée.

Cell Group B

Pour Louise et Denise Goulet
l'hiver est la saison préférée.
parce que tous les samedis,
les deux filles
vont faire du ski.
Elles adorent
les montagnes au nord
où elles font ce sport.
pour se préparer.
Malheureusement,
il faut faire la queue longtemps
quand on loue son équipement.
Denise a dit, "J'espère
être intermédiaire!"
En haut des pistes
il est très triste
parce que Denise Goulet
est tombée.
Elle s'est fait mal. Où?
au genou.
Autour d'un feu de bois
on boît du chocolat.
Denise ne veut pas aller à l'infirmerie.
Donc, Raymond a cherché le moniteur qui
est leur ami.
Denise a marché un peu,
tout en disant "Ça va mieux!"

Cell Group C

C'est la saison de ski,
et Louise dit "Allons-y!"
Quand il ne fait pas trop mauvais,
et la neige est parfaite,
avec skis, bâtons et lunettes,
les filles et M. Goulet
vont aller à Saint-Sauveur.
Ils arrivent à une heure.
Pour remonter les pistes,
elles ont pris le télésiège.
Denise s'est élancée très vite, et

Cell Group D

Quelle saison est-ce que vous préférez?
Pour moi, c'est l'été.
Mais pour les filles Goulet,
l'hiver, c'est leur saison préférée.

Les deux filles
vont faire du ski
tous les samedis.

Les deux soeurs
skient à Saint-Sauveur.

elle est tombée dans la neige.
Denise est devenue très triste.
Louise l'a aidée à se relever,
et elles sont descendues au chalet
où elles ont trouvé un feu de bois,
et avec leurs amis ont bu du chocolat.
Raymond a cherché un moniteur qu'il a
toute sa vie connu,
parce que Denise a mal au genou.
Il a vérifié
que rien n'est cassé.
Louise et Denise ont une bonne journée.

Elles achètent leurs billets
et vont au chalet
pour se préparer.

Denise et Louise regardent la neige
sur la montagne du télésiège.

Denise Goulet
est tombée
parce qu'elle est partie
trop vite, et elle dit
"Le ski? C'est fini."
Les filles sont allées au chalet
pour se préparer.
Elles sont arrivées
et Raymond est allé
pour chercher
le moniteur
de Saint-Sauveur.
Autour d'un feu de bois
ils boivent du chocolat
Mais Denise n'en veut pas.
Là-bas sur la piste
Denise était très triste.
Mais autour du feu
ça va mieux.

SPANISH CLASSES: I. EN LA PLAYA

Camino pies descalzos
mirando a chicos guapísimos.
En mi barco puedo flotar
y brinco en el agua para refrescar.
Nado debajo de los barcos con aletas
y miro las cosas con caretas.
El sol está muy brillante
y el día muy caliente.
Yo tengo mi toalla
para descansar en la playa.
Miro a un muchachito
navegando su barquito.

En el mar frío
tomo un botecito.
Necesito una silla para
descansar en la orilla.
Muchas palmeras son lindísimas
pero otras no son bellísimas.
En algunos veleros del mar
hay personas que aprenden a navegar.

II. LA COMIDA (Spanish I class)

Yo como mucho flan,
pero no como pan.
Me gusta el jamón.
No me gusta el limón.
Me gustan los moles
porque tienen frijoles.
Como mucho chocolate
en el restaurante.
Después de comer la cena
yo dejo una propina.
Entonces voy a la frutería
para comprar más sandía.

II. EL MEDIO AMBIENTE (Spanish II)

Es nuestra responsabilidad
para salvar la ciudad.
El espacio está muy sucio.
porque tiene mucho desperdicio.
El ambiente es impuro.
Necesitamos hacerlo limpio.
El ambiente
Se ensucia fácilmente.
Es importante
que en nuestra generación
paremos la erosión.

III. CUIDAR LA TIERRA (SPANISH II)

No me gusta contaminar
Prefiero reciclar
A muchas personas les gusta fumar
pero no puedo respirar.
Si no sabe lo que la industria crea
le aconsejo que usted lo lea.
Es la responsabilidad de toda la gente
limpiar el mundo rápidamente.
No pienso que usted quiera
el Universo sin Tierra

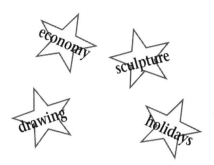

Part Three

CULTURE

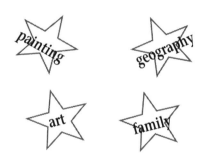

MUSEUM WALL

PURPOSE: To feature topics of a cultural nature

INTRODUCTION: This is adaptable to postcard collections, posters, or photographs to teach geography. A museum wall of newspaper pages is also a novel and effective way to teach cultural aspects. Such an activity provides a highly enjoyable way of simulating a museum experience for art lessons. Students enjoy being able to walk around, at their leisure, to ask questions of the teacher, and to linger at what catches their fancy.

To make this activity purposeful, the students should be given a handout with some basic information, and some questions to which they must respond. This activity could take on the tenor of a treasure hunt to heighten students' interest in observing more acutely.

Consider your classroom a museum!

TO TEACH GEOGRAPHY

1. Using staples, thumb tacks, or masking tape, attach the pictures to the walls, chalkboard, door, and possibly, the windows of the classroom.

2. Organize the pictures according to one area so as not to mix geographical areas. All pictures of the south of France should be together. Pictures of the Loire Valley go together. Pictures of Paris go together. The geography of the class will help establish the geography of the country.

3. Move the chairs out of the way, or group them in the center of the classroom to promote accessibility to the pictures.

4. A guide or follow-up sheet might include questions such as: In which part of France would you find the following: a. the Alps b. the capital c. Roman aqueducts.

The travel section of the local newspaper often features wonderful articles and alluring pictures of the Caribbean islands, and of the many countries in South and Central America. These articles may be preserved by laminating them, a tactic especially useful where there are scenic pictures.

In previewing each article, you should scan it for salient points of interest, then underline or highlight just the target sentences or paragraphs. It is intended that students read only the target information of each article, write down the information on their guide sheets or "treasure hunt" sheets, then move on to the next item. An awkward situation occurs when students try to read the whole article on the wall. If students want to read the whole article, you could copy it for them.

TO TEACH SOCIAL ISSUES AND CUSTOMS

During the holidays, some students or teachers may have the opportunity to travel to places where foreign languages are spoken, and that they could bring back a newpaper in that language. Student trips to Puerto Rico and to the Dominican Republic—to name a couple of places—provide wonderful, vicarious, cultural learning experiences.

1. Cut out full pages of the newspaper, circle pertinent items with a yellow highlighter, then attach the papers to the walls.

2. Circle words or highlight phrases that students might know.

3. Circle prices, current movies being shown, times, dates, advertisements, products, foods, weather prognostications, real estate notices, jokes, and comics.

4. Circle social or human events, for example, announcements of births, deaths, weddings, sweet sixteen celebrations, "quinceañeras," holiday celebrations, religious and patriotic holidays.

5. Circle vocabulary relating to economic, geographic, political, and social problems.

6. Circle sports events and all pertinent vocabulary.

7. Prior to having students walk around the classroom, distribute a handout asking them to find certain items and to offer their personal reactions or questions about what they have viewed.

TO TEACH ART APPRECIATION

This display could feature the work of one artist, or the work of one famous artist per century, or the works of artists within a specific movement.

Most students are not trained to judge art, or even to recognize the exciting elements of it. Guide their attention by focusing their viewing, and by eliciting their answers to questions about colors, shapes, symbols, figures, emotions, and other elements.

1. Using works of art from calendars, postcards, or books, laminate them if possible to preserve them, since students often feel compelled to touch the paintings. Museums sell beautiful calendars of particular artists!

2. Number the works as if they were in a museum. Bright-colored triangles of paper can be used for numbering the works. Attach the triangles to a bottom corner of each work.

3. Make a few bright-colored signs identifying the painter, the century he or she lived in, and any other particulars of importance. Such information may include the names of styles or periods, such as "surrealism" or "blue period."

4. Students should have in hand a sheet or packet of information and questions about their personal responses to the art. Ask students to interview one other student to solicit another's opinion of the artist's work.

5. This assignment can be further enhanced by appropriate homework.

SAMPLE HOMEWORK ASSIGNMENT

Based on a museum wall of Miró—with all the quirky figures—students should be given a list of 10 target language words (i.e., dog, cat, horse, shoes, store, bored, hungry, tired, eat, sleep) including nouns, verbs, and adjectives—or other language parts for upper-level classes. Students are instructed to write a fantasy story or paragraph, then to design, or sketch, the story as if Miró were sketching it. They should incorporate the quirky twists and shapes that demonstrate observation of his work. This can be adapted to many levels of language classes.

The following day, students should read one another's work and look at the Miró-like illustrations. This can be done in a circle, or students can pass their work to a neighbor. The work should be exchanged again, with at least a second student, to increase exposure to the many different and creative ways in which people recombine words to create ideas.

SAMPLE ART QUESTIONS

MIRO

born in the year: _____ died: _____
born in the town and country of: _____

What school, or schools, of art did he belong to?_____

_____

The newspaper articles describe Miró as "quirky." Go to the teacher's desk to find the definition of this word, then write it below: _____

_____

Name a painting which you think might be considered "quirky." _____

_____

Why did you choose this painting?_____

_____

The articles mention that surrealists delved into the subconscious as a source for their art. Why did they do this? _____

_____

Comment on the colors Miró used. _____

_____

Picture 10 was painted in 1937. Are you surprised by the colors he used, or the effect of them? _____

If yes, then why? _____

_____

Describe the figures in Miró's work. _____

_____

_____

Certain symbols or doodles are repeated in these works of art. Can you sketch some of them below?

Does Miró communicate any emotion to you through his work? _____

_____

What is your emotional response to Miró's work? _____

_____

Briefly discuss one painting with a classmate. List that person's comments. __

_____

_____

_____

SAMPLE GEOGRAPHY QUESTIONS BASED ON NEWSPAPERS

<u>COSTA RICA</u>

capital: _____ currency: _____

northern neighbor: _____

southern neighbor: _____

Selva Verde: What would you see there? _____

The article mentions "sloths." Consult the dictionary at the teacher's desk for the meaning of "slothful" _____

What is the correlation between "sloths" and "slothful"? _____
_____

What other types of fauna (animals) are there in Costa Rica? _____
_____

According to the article, plants and animals are interdependent. How is this true in the rain forest of Costa Rica? _____
_____

<u>BOLIVIA</u>

Name this famous lake, once sacred to the Incas. _____
What did J. Cousteau discover below the surface of this lake? _____
_____

Looking at the map of Bolivia, how easy is it to ship products to and from Bolivia? _____ Why? _____
_____
_____

How might this affect the economy of the country?_____
_____
_____

Many critical thinking questions can evolve from this type of assignment, thus it can be adapted to all levels of ability, from very basic to very advanced. It can also become the source of an interdisciplinary assignment, which can be expanded into science, economics, history, or art lessons.

SAMPLE VOCABULARY ASSIGNMENT FROM NEWSPAPERS

Find the following vocabulary words:

microwaves: _____ gas stove: _____

freezer: _____ bankruptcy: _____

mortgages at low cost: _____

compact discs: _____

When is the McDonald's special offer over? _____

What word tells you that? _____

NOTES

NOTES

NOTES